The Adventures of a £10 Pom Family

by

Barrie 'Yorkie' Joyce

Dedication and Acknowledgements

I wrote this account for my grandchildren and great grandchildren, to give them a feel for what life was like for their dad, grand and great grandparents in the late 1960s, and of course an idea of what it was like to live in Australia.

I am very grateful to Ann, one of my wife's lovely carers, who encouraged me to put pen to paper one day when I was telling her about one of my Australian adventures.

"It makes an interesting story,"' she said, "why don't you write it down?" I spoke to my future ghostwriter who told me to give it a go, and so I did. Twelve months later here it is!

I wrote this account fifty plus years after the events happened and acknowledge that time will have distorted my memories of the conversations recalled in this story. However, although a few words here-and-there will be different to those spoken all those years ago, the gist of their meaning is true, as are all the events described in this story of a two-year period of our lives.

Written by me, Barrie 'Yorkie' Joyce with support from my ghostwriter / editor / book cover and layout designer, Dawn Geatches. Thanks also to Marion for her helpful comments and editorial advice.

Disclaimer

If I have caused any offence due to the use of language or descriptions of attitudes prevalent at the time, I am sorry, but to paint an authentic picture of the times we lived in, I felt I needed to include warts and all.

PROLOGUE

In 1945, following the end of the Second World War, the Government of Australia initiated the Assisted Passage Migration Scheme in an attempt to boost Australia's population, and provide workers to support the country's booming industries. The migrants were charged ten pounds (about £150 in 2023) for their subsidised passage by air or ship, and in return were promised affordable housing, better jobs and a better way of life than faced them in post-war Britain. For those who made the trip, the reality, however, was somewhat different. The scheme continued until 1982, with an estimated one million British migrants arriving in Australia by 1972.

The term 'POM' is a corruption of the phrase 'Prisoner Of Mother England', referring to Britain's historical practice of sending convicted criminals to its Australian colony.

CONTENTS   PAGE

CONTENTS   **PAGE**

CONTENTS   PAGE

CHAPTER 1

Should we stay or should we go?

Oh no, not more rain! I wondered back in that early part of 1967 if it would ever end; little did I know that soon I would be longing for a spell of 'bad' weather. Margaret and I had been married nearly seven years and our son Dale had just turned seven. Blimey, we were so young, childhood sweethearts married at 17 and 19 and now we both worked full-time, Margaret at a local print-firm and me, I worked for the council building and laying roads.

We lived in a rented house in Hull in an area classed as 'slum housing'. We expected that in a couple of years we would be moving into a newly built council house, and all the signs for this were good until the council put all house building on hold for another year or two. In the meantime, we kept hearing and reading about the £10 Australian Emigration Scheme, and gradually we began to dream about life in the sunshine. Eventually, Margaret requested the application forms, we filled them out and popped them in the post box at the top of our street, never believing we would hear any more about Australia.

Another four weeks of heavy rain went by then one day on returning from work we found an official looking envelope in our hallway. It was a reply from Australia House London, requesting more information about ourselves and the reasons for wanting to emigrate. The letter took us by surprise because we never expected to hear anything more about emigrating; that sort of thing didn't happen for people like us. Gradually, excitement began to build and with it a conflict arose: should we send for more information and take a few more steps along this path, or should we forget all about it and make the best of what we had? Every time one of us thought we should 'shut-up and put-up' the other said we had nothing to lose; my mum died in 1962 and Margaret's parents both died within 11 days of each other in 1966, and what a huge shock that was! So we were 'free agents' in that respect, with no elderly parents to look after. We sent for more information about the emigration scheme.

Another few weeks later saw more letters arrive with details of the scheme. Margaret carefully followed the instructions and sent off our wedding and birth certificates. That's when our lives began to feel unreal because the application process was becoming serious. We did our best to carry on with our everyday lives, working, shopping, taking trips to the countryside and especially the seaside, but at the back of our minds Australia beckoned. A long time seemed to go by with no news until one day a thick envelope landed on the doormat. It contained instructions for the three of us to go for an all-expenses-paid medical exam, including several vaccinations, one of which made us feel quite ill. Sometimes, it was difficult to contain our growing excitement when we thought about travelling to a new land and a new life, and at other times all three of us felt very scared and worried about it all.

After the jabs we just had to wait for further instructions about the next steps. Both of our families were upset when we told them about emigrating, especially one of Margaret's nieces, Roslyn, because we were all very close. Then we received a letter from our local council informing us that before the end of 1967 we would be rehoused in a new property on the outskirts of Hull. This news threw us into a tizz and once again made us question what we were doing - had we thought it all through properly? At the same time information from Australia described how, by working hard, we would be able to own our own bungalow with land. And of course, there was the year-round sunshine, so we continued with the emigration process.

By this time, having sailed through the medicals, we knew we had been accepted but we had no leaving date. All that was left for us to do was to make arrangements about what we were going to take and find a removal firm that would ship all of our chosen worldly goods to the other side of the world. We found Pickfords and, after we had sorted what we could sell from what would be coming with us, Pickford's removals took over and boxed and stored the lot. By then, information about our moving dates arrived and we got a date in September 1967. Once again doubts about emigrating arose but we pressed on.

The photo shows one of my older sisters, Elsie, her husband, Bill, Margaret and Dale on a trip together before we left for our Big Adventure. It was taken in the days before animal welfare laws protected animals from being used as photo 'props,' and needless to say, we didn't know any better at the time.

About a week before we were due to set off to London for the start of our Australian adventure, we handed in our notices at work. This was really happening! Then the time came to say goodbye to my sisters, our extended family and our friends at the railway station, and oh my, what a sad time that was. Tears and hugs all round until we had to pull ourselves away and board the train.

We headed to London to spend a couple of days with one of Margaret's older sisters, Edie and her family in Brixton. The journey took over four hours and I spent most of it looking through the rail carriage windows, absorbing as much of England as I could to take with me to our new life in Australia. As we chugged along, the sky changed from heavy grey clouds full of rain to light and fluffy clouds wafting across the blue late summer skies with its glimpses of waning sunshine. I said to Margaret what a good omen this was for the start of our new lives.

Before long we pulled into King's Cross station and were met by Edie and family with a taxi waiting to whisk us away to Brixton. Edie cooked us a lovely meal and the occasion was both happy and sad, especially for Margaret. We slept soundly that night and felt we were having a mini holiday before our big adventure. Even at this late stage we were unsure about what we were doing and if we were making the right decision for us

9

all, but I thought of the flock of birds flying in V-formation I'd seen from the train and knew that, as long as I had Margaret and Dale either side of me, I could keep us all safe and on course to make the best of our new life.

Forty-eight hours later with passports, air tickets and all our documents in-hand, the three of us boarded the huge 747 and found our seats. None of us had ever flown before and I will never forget the monstrous roar of the engines as the plane taxied along the runway. I clasped Margaret's hand, and she clasped Dale's. "We can do this" I whispered over and over as the plane rose effortlessly into the air. Every seat on the plane was occupied by us '£10 Poms' all escaping to the land of sunshine.

There were two stops enroute: the first in Istanbul and the second in Bombay for refuelling. We seemed to be tired for the whole journey and welcomed the chance to disembark in Bombay. On leaving the plane the heat nearly knocked us off our feet; there was no bright sunshine, but it was very humid. We were also shocked to see many poor souls begging and climbing into wastebins to see what they could scavenge. We came from a poor area in Hull, but this was poverty on a whole new level. After a few hours in the airport we were allowed back on the 747 and felt like we had experienced our first mini adventure, in paying a brief but eye-opening visit to Bombay, India.

CHAPTER 2

The arrival: What happens now?

Thirty-six hours after leaving London we finally touched down at Perth airport, Western Australia. We were met by the Australian Emigration Authorities and taken by taxi to begin our new life at an Migrant's Hostel called 'Graylands'. I was feeling a mix of worry, excitement and fear at having left my home of twenty-seven years and willingly taken my family into the Big Unknown. The three of us were too tired and jet-lagged to pay much attention to the land we drove through on our journey to Graylands. And our initial impressions of Australia didn't develop until we had spent the first few weeks getting used to our new surroundings and exploring the city of Perth, which was about five miles (eight kilometres) from Graylands.

Life at Graylands Camp took some getting used to, it was a bit like a very basic holiday camp where you had to go to work. We, like many of the families on camp lived in a Nissen hut with a typical corrugated and domed iron roof, which meant there was no escape from the heat even at night, when the temperature could still be above 70°F (21°C).

The huts were very basic and disappointing - we'd left more luxury behind in Hull, in our soon-to-be-condemned 'slum' home. The huts had a simple layout with one room that served as the living space containing a small kitchen area, and there was only one separate bedroom. The kitchen had a sink and cooker, a table and two chairs; the bedroom, a double bed and a wardrobe, and the living room one settee that Dale used at night as his bed. There was no bathroom in the huts, everyone traipsed over to the shower and toilet blocks. At night we used a bucket instead of venturing outside to the toilets. At least there was electricity, and when at night we drew the curtains over the three windows and switched on the lights, the hut looked quite cosy. We soon began to see it as our new home; after all, apart from each other it was all we had.

This photo of Nissen huts on Graylands was taken in 1951. They were the same when we arrived in 1967. (Image slwa_b6765516_2:BA3306/21 Sourced from the collections of the State Library of Western Australia and reproduced with the permission of the Library Board of Western Australia)

For our meals everyone went to the canteen where we could choose the food we'd been used to, only better because we never ate steak in Hull, it was too expensive. At Graylands we could eat it every day if we wanted, and chips. Dale loved the puddings and custard, and Margaret loved the pineapple - she was a bit more adventurous in her choices than I was.

When we first arrived on Graylands everyone was issued with a knife, fork and spoon and were told we shouldn't lose nor forget to take them along to the canteen at mealtimes. Of course, Dale continually forgot his and was refused a meal, so he had to sit and watch us eat and pick food from our plates. The amount of food wasted from the canteen was terrible and happened because the portion sizes were too large for most of us Brits, we weren't used to it. The noise in the canteen was worse than at a Billy Butlins holiday camp, so we used to save the food we couldn't eat and take it back to our huts to eat the following day, to reduce the number of times we went to the deafening canteen.

In a few short weeks, Dale and I found we loved travelling to Perth because we went there by steam train, which always felt exciting. We also soon found that everything was more expensive than in the UK and I remember Margaret said the washing powder was very, very expensive, although fortunately it lasted a long time because the sunshine bleached all our clothes white anyway.

Dale fitted in well at his new school, a short distance from Graylands Camp, and was soon walking to it – barefoot. A lot of the kids did the same and the teachers never seemed to mind. He also joined in a lot of the activities on the camp: football, cricket, rounders, and his favourite was when the school went to the lido in the local Swan River.

As time went by we met some very nice fellow 'Poms', all hoping to make a better life for their families: Gerry, Lil and family from Liverpool; Ray and family from Bradford; Tony and family from Manchester; Taffy and his wife from Wales; a family from Scotland and many more. Maybe it was just me, but it seemed like we felt we were all in this together, there was safety, security and sanity in numbers. I mean, if so many of us had made the choice to move here it couldn't be a mistake, could it?

My work in Britain on the council highways, building roads, driving the diggers, compressors and the massive roller that flattened the tarmac, meant that after a couple of weeks I got an interview with a firm laying new footpaths and making new roads. The firm was about 20 miles (32 kilometres) from Graylands, and I travelled there by (steam) train. The working conditions were terrible – no health and safety measures at all, no unions were allowed, and you were lucky to find a water tap. The sun beat down on us all day, and we were covered in dust from the start of the shift to the end. This was a huge shock to my body! I was roasted like a chestnut by the end of my first day, returning home with a deep tan. A few days later I began to think wistfully about the rain we'd left behind, falling in Hull. Bloody hell, what had we done?

CHAPTER 3

Our first experience of an Australian Spring and my first job in the 'Outback'

We left the UK just when autumn was making an appearance and we landed in Australia at the start of spring when temperatures averaged about 90 °F (approximately 30 °C). I worked in a gang of six, and not one of us was a white Australian or 'Aussie' as I would have called them back in 1967. In my gang were a couple of native Australians – Aborigine men - and after a couple of weeks working with them, I was called into the office and asked if I was racist with them. The thing is, I didn't really know what 'racist' meant at that time, and over fifty years later I still have no idea what the meeting was about. Us migrants were called "Pommie Bastards" by some of the white Australians, was that a form of racism? I never thought about it beyond realising that us immigrants and Aborigine men were there to do the heavy work the white Australians didn't want. I didn't stay much longer with that firm. Even the offer of being promoted to 'Ganger' where I'd be in charge of the team and their work with higher pay, didn't persuade me to stay.

Spring was progressing towards Summer and with it the temperature was rising day-by-day. We needed to buy some summer clothes: shorts, lightweight tops, plimsolls and flipflops, and wide-brimmed hats or baseball caps to shade our eyes. The heavy jumpers and raincoats we arrived wearing were stored at the back of the wardrobe. One weekend Margaret and Dale decided they wanted to go see the sea, which meant walking to the nearest beach - Cottesloe. We heard from our new friends it was a couple of miles from Graylands but we didn't really know where it was.

We set off walking early one morning thinking we were being very sensible. After a couple of hours of plodding along dusty tracks in the ever-increasing heat we were completely lost. There were no buses to be seen and only the odd car passed us. Eventually, we admitted defeat - we were lost and knew we needed to turn back before it got any hotter and we got even more lost. This was our first realisation that being ill-prepared in this environment and weather could have serious consequences. On the positive side, just as exhaustion was starting to overwhelm us we saw a large green iguana, about two feet (about 60 centimetres) from nose to tail. We'd never seen anything like it before and although we were a bit scared and gave it a wide berth, we, especially Dale, were fascinated by the lovely creature basking in the sunshine. Our new discovery pepped us up enough to find our way back to Graylands.

I soon learnt that to earn decent wages I would need to work away from home and get a job in 'The Outback' – the area outside the populated areas, where not much happened beyond nature being nature. One of the few sources of employment there was in the opencast iron ore mines. I teamed up with Taffy and Brummie - back then we called our mates by where they came from (and being from Yorkshire I became 'Yorkie') because somehow this seemed important to us - and away we went to build a new railway line. We were flown in a light aircraft to the mine about 400 miles (640 kilometres) north of Graylands. On site there were blokes from all nations, and we all bunked at the accommodation site in corrugated huts. The living accommodation was basic, but the food was very good with steak, chips, meat pies and gravy, but not many vegetables or fruit. It was food to feed the muscles to keep us doing the hard physical work.

Each day we were driven the three miles (five kilometres) from our dorms to the worksite, ready to start work by 7am so we could finish before it got too hot to work. The three of us stuck together and our job was to lay sleepers (called 'props') for the railway track and to do it fast. The company supplied us with some work-wear - very wide-brimmed hats hung with tassels to keep the flies away. They weren't very effective, but it didn't take us long to get used to the flies buzzing around our heads and hovering around our sweat-soaked bodies. Every hour a water wagon came on site and drove round to each gang, and no-one missed the chance to take a long swig of cold, life-saving water. We knew when the wagon was on its way by blokes shouting 'Water on! Water on!' What a relief to hear those words! I thought at the time I'd never take water for granted ever again.

Now I wonder at the change in what became important in just a few short weeks. In England we were thinking about moving to our own house with an indoor bathroom and garden, and we went backwards and forwards to our jobs in an environment that - we knew without being aware of it - wouldn't kill us. A few weeks later we were in a land where the weather could kill us, water became precious to us, and we were living in a corrugated oven. But we adapted and everything was new, even if much of it was dangerous and uncomfortable. Never did Margaret and I ever imagine we would one day travel to a country and make a life on the other side of the world, and yet that's what we had done. And that was enough of an achievement to help us adapt. I can see this all now but of course at the time we were just getting on with our new lives.

The railway line was being laid from the opencast mine near the northern coast at Port Hedland to link to the main lines taking the iron ore to Perth. Taffy, Brummie and me, we worked seven-hour shifts on a stretch of line about 20 miles (32 kilometres) long, and by 2pm we were finished before it became too hot to work. Without the water wagon coming round every hour, we wouldn't have lasted a day! At the end of our shift, we were glad to climb into the utility vehicle or 'ute' - a kind of pick-up truck with an open back, the main type of motor vehicle over there - and trundle back to camp where we would stand in line to use the outdoor showers. These were cobbled together from canopies of corrugated sheet metal with a drum of cold water on top that was released by yanking the chain attached to the bucket. The sun-warmed water gushing over the corrugated sheets produced the shower for the naked bloke standing underneath the edge of the canopy.

I tried to estimate how many workers there were on site, but I don't remember how many Italian, German, French and Polish men there were, and guessing was difficult because we all mostly kept to ourselves until mealtimes when we all went to the site canteen. There must have been a few hundred of us. On site there were a couple of generators that kept the food as cool as possible. Taffy, Brummie and me, we heard that every month a light plane arrived from Perth with stores of goods such as soaps, cans of beers and some food we couldn't get every day in the canteen. Letters arrived along with the stores and about six workers arrived per flight, with six returning to Perth in exchange. At that time there were no mobile phones and no telephone boxes in sight, so we all looked forward to the letters arriving. We noticed there were no white Australians on site until the pilots of the light planes arrived – this brought it home to me that us migrants were doing the jobs the white Aussies didn't want to do.

After a week and a half of heavy graft Taffy, Brummie and me, we decided we wanted to go back home and wanted to be three of the six on the next flight out, partly because we missed our families back at Graylands, and partly because we were worn down by the heat, flies, and general conditions. I worked for one day at the face of the iron ore mine on a small digger (or bobcat) loading up dumper trucks, but that was no better than laying the props - there was no escape from the heat and flies and there were bonus clouds of dust generated by digging and dumping.

We made enquiries about the next flight to Perth and were gutted to be told the flight was fully booked. We needed to rethink our plan so when we heard that another ute from another site was heading back to Perth in a couple of days, we got ready to say goodbye to the prop-laying. When the ute arrived a couple of Polish chaps joined us and squeezed themselves into the tiny space at the back. One of the Polish workers was called Bruno, and although I didn't know it then, we were to work together on many jobs. We made a great team and clicked straight away on our long, bumpy journey across the outback. Eventually, Graylands came into view and my heart almost burst with a combination of relief and happiness at the thought of being only a few minutes away from Margaret and Dale. For the eleven days we worked at the iron ore mine we were paid for only seven because we walked off the site. I didn't mind, better to have less pay than still be there grafting away, covered in flies and choking on dust.

CHAPTER 4

I get a job in high places and the use of a vehicle for daytrips

Margaret and I made great friends with a family from Liverpool (Gerry and Lil) and we would keep in touch for many years to come. As time went on the heat became more and more unbearable and we wanted to be by the sea. We eventually managed to find Cottesloe Beach, which was about a three-mile drive from Graylands, when Gerry and family took us in their car. It was a lovely spot with a lot of Poms sprawled on the white sandy beaches, with some of them venturing into the beautiful, bluey-green sea, soon to be joined by Dale and me. We'd never before seen the sea this colour – we were more used to the muddy brown of the North Sea off the East Yorkshire coast.

Margaret got a job as a domestic worker in a local psychiatric hospital, not far from the hostel. I needed to work too of course, and I got a tip there was a roofing job going in Perth with a firm called 'NuRoof'. The dollars weren't great but at least it was money coming in. I learnt that this firm was owned by a religious group that had works in other states across the country. My job was to work with hot bitumen to lay felt on roofs, and there was many a time I got blisters from handling it. There wasn't much in the way of health and safety measures in those days. After a few weeks the roofing firm let me occasionally take the ute home, but not before I passed a written exam to convert my UK driving licence into an Australian licence.

Margaret and Dale were settling in now and before long we were heading towards the end of the year. Looking back this was the longest time I had worked closer to home, and life in our new country was falling into a routine, just like in the UK. Margaret made a friend at work, called Carol, whose parents had emigrated many years ago from Hull. Their friendship grew and we used to visit Cottesloe Beach together with Carol and her husband, Neville, and they welcomed us into their home to share a few meals. Margaret was a bit upset that we couldn't invite them back to our home, but we didn't have the space nor the furniture to entertain anyone.

The utility vehicle or 'ute' I used when working for NuRoof and was allowed to take home at the weekends.

Working for the roofing company was also the only time I had a white Aussie workmate, and he went by the name of 'Big Bill'. He loved his grog (alcohol in general) and minis (beers) and drank more of them day-by-day, which made me glad I never had to work away with him. By 2pm each day it was too hot to work and we were either sitting in the shade of the truck or heading back to the depot. I did most of the driving, dropping him off at the nearest bar before we got back to the yard. From there I walked to the station to catch a stream train back to Graylands.

Big Bill wasn't a talker and there was just one time I remember him coming alive when I went to move the rolls of felt and suddenly, swift-as-anything, found Big Bill looming over me with a pickaxe. For a second my heart skipped a beat, then he swung the axe beyond me and down onto the snake that was resting by the rolls: "chop", "thud" and one snake became two - halves.

"You Pommie Bastards never learn!" he bawled and after that he became more friendly, even wanting to know what part of Britain I was from. "Yorkshire? Is it barren mate? Many Gum Trees?"

I said, "No Bill, none of them there, nowt but lush green fields, lovely cool woods and waterfalls a-plenty!" At least, that's how I pictured my beloved Yorkshire at that moment. I wondered what the hell I was doing in this barren land with snakes - bloody snakes that could kill! I'd been bitten by a grass snake on Ilkley Moor (maybe because I wasn't wearing a hat) and that was bad enough. But the moment of panic passed, and I told Bill there were regions in the UK called 'counties' and that each county had a slang word for its people, and that being from Yorkshire we were 'Yorkies'. Then I saw a rare sight – a smile creeping across his face - as he came out with, "All right mate, from now on you're a Pommie Yorkie Bastard!" Thanks, Big Bill, I think this meant we were Aussie mates!

On reporting for details of my next job I was called into the office and told that Big Bill would no longer be my workmate – he'd been sectioned at the local psychiatric hospital. This unsettled me because it was probably the same hospital where Margaret worked. Nothing more was said at that time. My new workmate was a Polish chap who was happy being called 'Richard' because his Polish name was a bit difficult for non-Poles to pronounce. Richard couldn't drive so I became our driver. We had a couple of weeks' work in the capital of the outback, called Kalgoorlie, nearly 400 miles (640 kilometres) from Perth. The work was to refelt a pub roof and a couple of other buildings. Richard was a nice chap, but we couldn't understand each other much and had to do a bit of improvised hand waving and miming. We lodged in a bed and breakfast in a shared room in a very small town (equivalent to a hamlet in the UK) about three miles (five kilometres) from Kalgoorlie.

One evening we decided to go to the bar for a couple of minis and to our surprise came across a gang of felters from the same firm as us. One of the gang I recognised straight away as Bruno, and it was great to see him again. We all got chatting and Bruno translated for Richard and me and everything was going well when we heard a lot of shouting in the back room, where there was a smaller bar. I would never have believed it if I hadn't seen it with my own eyes; there were four blokes at each end of the bar focusing all their attention along the bar length, willing their lucky cockroach to cross the finishing line first. It looked to me like serious fistfuls of dollars were changing hands. I wondered what made the cockroaches scuttle from one end to the other and found out they were attracted by the strong smelling leaves the gamblers placed at the end of the bar. Bruno, Richard and me, we all held on tight to our dollars and left the fellas to their 'roach game.

Those working days started early and finished early giving Richard and me a bit of free time, so we took the ute and went off the main track into the outback. Richard had been in the area before and directed me to a place where there were about a dozen emus grazing. They were an amazing sight, I'd never seen one before in my life, not even a drawing or a photo. Their necks were long and scrawny and their bodies very fluffy and balanced on two very long legs, which made them about six feet (two metres) tall. If only I'd had my box Kodak camera with me.

Richard told me a sad story about Big Bill, and we must have understood each other a bit more by then because I gleaned that since the last time Big Bill and I had worked together, he'd lost the plot and stabbed a fellow resident at the hostel for alcoholics, and that's the reason he was sectioned. The hospital he'd been sent to was where Margaret worked, which worried me a lot. One time when we worked together, Big Bill was disoriented, mumbling about the heat and his minis saying he didn't used to be like this years ago. In a way I felt sorry for him because I could see that working the way we did in the heat in this terrain it could be easy to lose the plot, especially if you didn't have any family and friends to love.

The work at the roofing firm became local for a few weeks and at the weekend I had use of the ute and took Margaret and Dale out-and-about, exploring the southern part of Perth. About six miles (ten kilometres) away lay Fremantle, where massive liners docked with their ships full of hopeful immigrants. Not far from the docks was a museum that was originally a prison for hundreds of convicts, mostly from the UK, and it gives me the shivers thinking about it - such a dark grey building, I wonder at the stories it could tell! We explored other areas around Perth including the coast and bought a surfboard for Dale and me to share. Some beaches were less crowded than others and finding them felt like finding treasure.

One day we went on a bus trip to see some underground waterfalls in the local caves. We made sure we visited as many of the tourist sites as we could fit in around our work schedules. Sometimes, we took Gerry and Lil's son with us because he and Dale had become good friends despite the two-year age gap. Some aspects of life in Australia took a bit of getting used to, some of them quite simple - such as shopping on a Saturday in Perth needed to be done by about midday, because after that everything - apart from the tourist attractions - closed until Monday morning. We were living a life similar to our life in the UK but with lots of sun, the use of a ute, plenty of new places to visit and adventures to be had. On the downside, we lived in a tin hut and we missed our families – pluses and minuses you might say.

On one of our weekend outings, we noticed boat trips sailing over the Swan River to a small area of land called 'Rottnest Island', and we booked a trip for the following Sunday. After crossing three miles (five kilometres) of a very choppy Swan River, we landed where we were greeted by hundreds of quokkas. They are members of the kangaroo family and look like large, fat, super-smiley squirrels with rat tails and miniature kangaroo arms and legs and a pouch, and although they're friendly to humans we were told they are wild animals and will bite, so definitely no touching nor feeding allowed.

There was a wooden hut on the island - noticeable because every other building we'd seen was made of tin – selling refreshing, ice-cold drinks, and we gratefully guzzled them down looking across the Indian Ocean, faces caressed by the breeze blowing across the white sands. The trees were abundant and thriving on Rottnest but there were no houses there because the island belonged to the quokkas. The trip back to Perth was quite calm, and not far from where we landed, I noticed a public swimming area and immediately clocked it as the destination for the following weekend's day trip.

Margaret and Dale standing on a rock in Rottnest Island with the Indian Ocean behind them; Dale feeding a friendly quokka (we weren't supposed to!)

CHAPTER 5

Spring becomes summer and along comes Sam

We began to notice that some of the Poms were no longer at Graylands, about half of them had moved off camp to live in their own houses and the other half had set sail back to the UK after living on Graylands for the allowed maximum of two years. Anyone returning to the UK before completing two years residency was obliged to pay the Australian government the full airfare that they had originally subsidised to entice migrants into the country.

Margaret was settling into her job but at times found it very unnerving because it was a psychiatric hospital. I was a bit worried when Richard told me that was where Big Bill was sectioned, but I think their paths never crossed. Sometimes, my imagination ran away with me.

The roofing firm had a couple of weeks work in the outback at Coolgardie, about 350 miles (560 kilometres) east of Perth. Richard didn't want the job so Bruno became my workmate, which suited me fine because he spoke more English. Bruno was not a drinker and said that those who were, were all fools spending all their money on grog. He described them as 'sun-freaks!' who emigrated to Australia only for the sunshine.

When Bruno was in the mood, we used to talk a lot about his family in Poland, including his parents. He was married and his wife was in the same situation with work – temporary contracts and low pay. 'We will never raise the fare to get back to Poland,' he used to say with tears in his eyes. He spoke about his home with its lush, green forests, waterfalls and streams and it sounded like the Yorkshire Dales. I promised myself there and then that I would not allow us to get trapped here, we needed to save money in case we wanted to go back home.

By now, it was well into late October which was mid-spring in Australia, and it was getting hotter day-by-day. I used to think of the weather in Hull and how the nights would be drawing-in. One of my older sisters, Elsie, regularly sent us letters keeping us up to date on what was going on in England.

I was back working close to Graylands at this time and one day I was approached by a chap working nearby who told me he was a sheeting-aluminium roofer, that there were just the two of them in his gang and most of the time he worked a lot further away from Perth. We got chatting and straight away I clocked him as a Cockney. Sam he was, he rented a house in Perth with his wife Maureen and their two daughters. We clicked when he told me that back in Blighty he did a lot of roofing work in Yorkshire, then he asked me if I was ever struggling for work to let him know and he'd get me fixed up.

"I don't think so Sam, not at the height you work at!"

"Don't worry about that, you soon get used to this kind of roofing!"

Sam showed me his caravan and said he'd bought it instead of paying for digs when away working, and so that he could take his family. I wondered why he had it with him on a job so close to home, and as if reading my mind, he opened the caravan door revealing some comfy-looking seats and a table topped with food and drink. He used it as a shelter and 'breakroom' from the unrelenting sunshine.

When I'd finished my work for the day, I strolled across to Sam's caravan and told him it was nice to have met him. He shook my hand and smiled, a twinkle in his eye.

"See you soon, Yorkie!"

I thought, *no bloody chance, Sam!*

For another few weeks I got roofing work around the suburbs of Perth. Sometimes, it was eerie because you didn't see many people out and about due to the heat, 'Only mad dogs and Englishmen....' was true over here! It was so damn hot! Everyone except migrant workers were indoors during the hottest parts of the day. I did many of the local jobs with Richard, and he used to talk about his native Poland. When I could understand him, it was funny to hear about his childhood; he said he would have loved to see London's Buckingham Palace and 'of course the Queen!'

Margaret often used to work weekends, which meant I got some free time with Dale. Me and a couple of other dads, we started to arrange cricket and football teams across the camp for the lads and we set-up regular games for them. There was no swimming pool on camp so we took it in turns to visit the nearest beach using whatever vehicles we had access to, sometimes piling as many kids as we could into the front and back of the ute. Good job we never came across any police, although they probably wouldn't have bothered much about safety back then.

One of the biggest problems in the Nissen huts was ants, we had thousands of them marching around and in and out of the huts in a huge line that was often accompanied by lines of kids marching alongside. Every few weeks or so a chap came around to spray the ants in an attempt to keep their numbers down, but it didn't work very well because they kept on marching. His job must have been like painting the Forth bridge - by the time he got round all the Nissen huts it was time to start again.

On November 5th not far from Graylands there was an organised bonfire with fireworks that were paid for by the council. Quite a lot of us Poms ventured out in the evening to see the bonfire and enjoy some minis at the beer stall. No-one wore a top-coat, scarf and woolly hat that early summer's evening. Instead, it was shorts and tassel-hats for this special Guy Fawkes night, although there wasn't a Guy Fawkes over there of course. This brought memories back for Margaret and me of the times we had gone to my (oldest) sister, Ivy's home in Swine - a little village near Hull - for bonfire night. We used to have jacket potatoes cooked in the bonfire, fireworks and fun in their large garden with all of Ivy's large family. Still, with the fireworks whizzing, cracking and popping and the fire blazing away, being outside at night away from the camp felt like a small adventure.

The next time I travelled away was for a couple of nights with Bruno and who should we run into but Sam. He came over to see us both.

"Now then Yorkie, I heard you were heading this way. Have you thought about changing jobs yet?"

I replied, "I'll meet you in the bar later on and will be on my own because Bruno doesn't drink." Our day's work finished around 3pm and I met Sam in the bar, he ordered us a couple of grogs. One thing of note about the bars was that in those days no women were allowed, it was men only, it's hard to believe now but it's true.

Sam told me that he and his family had been in Perth for about two years, and he did contract work for firms that specialize in corrugated sheet roofing. After a few more grogs we arranged to meet the next weekend in Perth at his house. He said he had a few weeks' work coming up soon, and we'd discuss it more at the weekend. Sam told me to bring Margaret and Dale to meet Maureen and his two daughters.

On the way home from the job, I told Bruno about the meeting I had with Sam and he said Sam was a 'good fella and a family man'. That's when I learnt that Sam also did some contract work for NuRoof. I noticed that Bruno didn't call Sam 'Pom' but used his name instead. I wasn't sure what that meant but felt Sam got Bruno's seal of approval and I trusted Bruno, so I felt I could trust Sam. I didn't know what Margaret would think of this new work adventure and was keen to hear her point of view. If she didn't want me to do it, I wouldn't. We'd shared everything and learnt that we needed to talk before making any big decisions. It hadn't always been that way!

A sad, longing feeling had started to creep over me during the last few weeks and I had to admit what it was - I was feeling homesick. I hoped this new work adventure with Sam would make this feeling go away, after all, I wanted to give living in Australia a chance of working for us. The prospects of making a good life were supposed to be high, that's what we'd been led to believe.

The following weekend, we three paid a visit to Sam and Maureen's home. It was good for Dale that he was between the ages of their two daughters, which meant he was a bit shy of the older one and a bit more relaxed with the younger one, which stopped him from getting too bossy or shy himself.

Sam offered me a job (that included working on high girder beams) fitting galvanized sheets to the roof and sides of metal skeleton frameworks of new buildings. Bricks weren't used because the buildings were on small industrial sites, and they needed to be constructed quickly. I had never worked at the height Sam was used to, but I said I'd have a go.

The next day Sam and family came over to Graylands to visit us. Sam said he would make it ok at NuRoof for me to work with him because he was sub-contracting from them, and he would 'put me on his books.' Until the first job with Sam came along, I would carry on working with Bruno hot bitumen felting.

CHAPTER 6

My first window cleaning job brings me a bucketful of trouble, and a ute is put to good use

I was lucky to have the use of one of NuRoof's utes at the weekends, and I drove Margaret and Dale into Perth to go shopping. That's where I saw an advert in a shop window: 'Window Cleaner wanted for Saturdays; all tools of the trade supplied! Call in here'. So, I did and left my details. I thought *in for a cent, in for a dollar!* I knew I could handle that sort of work because I'd done it back in the UK.

The following week a letter arrived at the camp's office addressed to 'Hut 129D.' Every letter we ever received there felt as exciting as receiving Christmas presents when I was a kid. The letter was about the window cleaning round and said if I was still interested to go along to the shopping arcade where I'd left my details and be there for 9am next Saturday. Margaret was working that weekend, so friends Gerry and Lil looked after Dale for a few hours, "as long" they said, "as he brings his knife, fork and spoon!"

I arrived before 9am and met a chap whose nationality I couldn't identify, and who spoke good English. The job was for four hours a week every Saturday morning, which helped to pass the time while Margaret was working, and Dale was busy playing football and swimming with his new mates and their dads. Fortunately, the windows I had to clean were in the shade of the arcade awning. Window ladders, cloths and buckets were all provided and I got to work straight away. When the job was finished, I was to leave the equipment at the back of the shop where I'd met the boss. He reappeared to pay me at 1pm when all the shops were closing for the weekend. I thought I was on to a good thing, earning a little extra money that we could save to build-up for either the deposit on a house over here, or, if things didn't work out, our return fare to the UK.

The next Saturday I turned up again and got my equipment from the back of the shop and got started. After a couple of hours one of the women working in the arcade shops asked me if I wanted a cold drink. *Bloody hell, yes,* I thought but answered, "Not half!" Without thinking, I downed tools and left the gear outside the shop and went inside to savour my drink. The shop staff were friendly, and they wanted to know all about Graylands, and where we were from in England. We got chatting away until eventually I said I had to get back to the job. Feeling refreshed and happy after the friendly chat, I was ready to get stuck in again and finish the job before the boss appeared to pay me.

"Oh, Christ, no!" I spat out on finding my tools weren't where I'd left them. Some bugger had nabbed them! I searched around the area but nothing – they'd gone! I hung around until the boss appeared and of course he didn't take the news well. He was trying to charge me for the cost of replacement ladders and cleaning stuff. Also, he said he'd pay a visit to Graylands to collect the cash as compensation for his lost equipment. He was bigger than me but not the biggest chap, and without thinking I said,

"You'd do well to remember I've got some big, strong, £10 Pom brothers there who'd love to meet you and tell you EXACTLY where to go!" That must have been enough bluff for him because he never did turn up at Graylands!

I later heard from the shop workers that I was the third window cleaner in a few weeks. I don't know what was going on there, maybe it was a scam – employ naïve immigrants, pay them one week's wages, 'steal' the equipment the next week and demand compensation from them? Maybe he got comp money more often than not, who knows, but he didn't get any from me!

One day Bruno told me to take the ute home after every shift and pick him up every morning before we went to the yard. This would be better than leaving it at the roofing-firm's yard at the end of every shift because it meant less time and money spent on train travel, plus it felt like I 'owned' a vehicle for the first time in my life. Having easy access to the ute came in handy several times especially when there was a family emergency.

Dale was adventurous, always trying to find out what was around the next corner and often went wandering by himself or with his mates. On one of his adventures, Dale and his pal were wandering over to the Ministry of Defence area outside Perth and not far from Graylands. He said he and his mate had been watching a couple of older teenagers searching about in the fields and wondered what they were looking for. Dale and pal then started to look around in the field and found lots of spent and bent bullets. Before they knew it, Dale had been hit in the head with one of the bullets fired from a catapult. He was very lucky - it could have hit his eye.

Somehow, his pal spotted a ranger and ran for help, the teenagers scarpered. The ranger picked Dale up who was almost but not quite, knocked out, and drove him and his pal back to camp. With Dale sat in between Margaret and me in the front seat of the ute, I drove to Perth hospital where he got a couple of stitches to the side of his head. This was one of those occasions when we were very grateful to have use of the ute, although I don't know what the hospital staff thought of a ute turning-up with a lot of buckets and materials covered in tar and a youngster bleeding from his head!

CHAPTER 7

Christmas in summertime!?

Summer was well underway which meant keeping in the shade as much as possible. We got a chance to see what effect this weather had on a typical suburban garden when Margaret received a dinner invitation from Carol and Neville. Their house was a new build in a new suburb and was a grand-looking bungalow, which was the style of most houses in suburbia. They didn't have much furniture beyond the bare minimum, which was the general trend at that time. The garden was bone-dry because there was always a water shortage in the summer and a ban on hosepipes, leaving gardens with patches of scorched earth and nothing growing, at least nothing I recognised.

Christmas was just around the corner and when Margaret had a weekend off, we went into Perth and bought some Christmas cards to send back home to England. I still thought of England as my home and wondered if that would ever change. There weren't many decorations and Christmas trees either for sale or hung up around the city.

We didn't yet know that the custom on Christmas Day was to spend it on the beach, lazing under large sun-umbrellas and surfacing only to cook the Christmas meal over barbecues. When we found out that's how the Australians spend Christmas, we did the same and joined a group going to the beach for the day. Some of the dads took over the barbecue and although there was no turkey there were plenty of steaks. That's when I got all nostalgic for 'Dear Old Blighty' where we would have seen lights in the centre of Hull City, shop window festive displays, and sometimes even snow on Christmas Eve, but maybe I was getting too sentimental. On Boxing Day a few of us from the camp returned to the beach, played a few team games, and went for a swim in the sea. This distracted me and made me feel better about being so far away from home at Christmas when we would have been visiting family.

CHAPTER 8

1968 begins and it's time for my first job away from home with Sam

Our first Christmas in Australia was over and January 1968 arrived. This was a quiet time at work so Bruno and I stayed in the yard depot cleaning and stock-checking. One time we were sent to the suburbs for a job, but first we had to call at Richard's house to meet one of the office-bods, Alec, to pick up the job details. Our employer was owned and run by a religious community whose name I never knew. We arrived at Richard's house before Alec and saw a tv switched on in the corner of the room. Alec arrived shortly after and on spotting the tv he started screaming.

"You, you will all end up in Hell!" *You mean we not there already?* I thought.

"You are all, evil, damned people!" He was getting quite distressed now. We turned around to face him and found he was trying to cover his ears and eyes, at the same time as backing out of the room as fast as he could, when he tripped, fell into the door and bashed his head leaving a bleeding gash across his forehead. Down he went and was out-for-the-count! Bruno nodded to me and with Richard's help we picked Alec up off the floor and laid him on the veranda outside in the shade.

"Don't let the devil catch you in your dreams, Alec!" I said, patting him on the shoulder. With that, we collected the paperwork and off we went to our next job.

A week or so later, it was time for my first job with Sam. We would work away from home for a couple of weeks on work sub-contracted from NuRoof. We travelled south from Perth about 260 miles (420 kilometres) to the whaling port of Albany, and although the journey wasn't long the roads were dust tracks and hellish bumpy. We booked into a hotel on the outskirts of Albany where we saw only one other visitor. He looked like John Wayne and even tied his horse to the wooden bar at the front of the hotel. The following day we scouted out where we'd be working, expecting delivery the same day of all of the roofing materials from a local firm.

The roofing job was on the docks where trawlers brought in dead whales to be butchered, and Oh God! the sights and smells were terrible. I'd never seen whaling up-close like this before, the closest I ever came was visiting Hull's Whaling Museum. But here, I could see huge creatures lying dead on the warehouse floors when only a few days before they were living in their pods gliding through the depths of the Indian Ocean with their families.

It was obvious Sam had been here before or somewhere like it because he took it all in his stride. I think he was trying to get me used to different types of jobs I would encounter when working with him. He brought along heavy-duty masks and gloves that helped protect us from the stench a bit, but nevertheless the foul smell penetrated the gear and lingered on our clothes and skin.

We started the job around 7am following a hearty breakfast at the hotel. Sam brought along enough fresh water to see us through the day's work. By the time we finished I think he was pleased with what we had achieved, not that he said as much but he did seem quite happy. We walked down to the whaling ships on the docks and I swear we'd walked onto the set of a horror film - the whales where being gutted and sawn into pieces. The pieces of whale meat were washed, frozen, and packed onto trucks for the Australian market. How the hell those blokes did that work was beyond me, the stench alone would be bad enough without all the blood and gore.

We were back at the hotel by mid-afternoon where there were decent shower facilities. As the day progressed, I felt the air getting cooler and the patches of grass dotted around the hotel grounds swayed in the breeze. Albany had a higher rainfall than Perth and was greener and more fertile. A stronger wind developed in the evening and thankfully blew the dead whale smell offshore.

I noticed there was a phone in the hotel which meant it was a 'Class 1' hotel. Sam arranged to use it to phone his wife and daughters most nights. I felt very lonely and lost because I couldn't contact Margaret and Dale and hear their familiar voices. Sam could tell how I was feeling and arranged with Maureen that before the next time they spoke she would have updated Margaret about our Albany adventures.

We usually had a couple of grogs in the evening, and a few nights into our trip I felt relieved and happy when Sam finished his call and told me

Margaret said everything was well and she was looking forward to me coming back home soon. We were getting on well with the job and I was getting used to the work, although it was all very new to me compared to what I did back in Blighty.

A few days later an even stronger smell of dead whale flesh filled the air. When we walked to the docks, we saw it came from an even larger whaling vessel than the first, which had already left on another hunting trip.

This type of roofing was a lot harder than felting with hot bitumen due to the conditions and the materials. Sam brought along a couple of pairs of eye-shields, a pair each to protect us from the sun's blinding reflections off the shiny, metal roof sheeting, but even with the shields it was sometimes impossible to see through the glare. When we finished the job a couple of Italian chaps had a word with Sam to offer us a few more days' work. Sam told me that everything would be arranged for us and that the materials would be ready and waiting, so I said 'why not, let's do it'. Sam told his wife we'd be back at Graylands in a few days and that she should tell Margaret.

The new job was a further 10 feet (three metres) higher up, but by then I didn't bat an eyelid at the extra height. The additional work was a job the tax man didn't get to know about! It was becoming clear to me that there were loads of opportunities to make 'unofficial' money if that's what you wanted, although I knew it was a route that Margaret wouldn't want us to go down.

One of the warehouse skeletons Sam and I covered in aluminium sheeting from top to bottom

CHAPTER 9

March to May is Autumn and with it comes a nice surprise

Following the job down in Albany, Sam and family became good friends. By now we were in March 1968, and became aware that the Immigration Authorities were beginning to pressure us migrants to start looking elsewhere (i.e., away from the camp) for housing. The time limit to stay at Graylands was two years, so when a land agent gave a talk in the canteen about a new housing development for bungalows a mile or so outside Perth, we went along to listen.

After attending the meeting, we paid a visit to the development. The land looked barren although the photos of the houses looked quite impressive. The deposit for a plot was quite large and many of us Poms couldn't afford it, the prices were out of most manual workers' reach. Fifty years later we might still be paying the mortgage for it! We never saw that land agent again on Graylands – he must have realised we weren't his target audience.

For a few months I was working at NuRoof, knowing that Sam had something else lined up for us and was just waiting to get the go-ahead with another contractor. One time while working with Bruno we finished early and he asked me if I'd like to meet his family. He lived in a very run-down area. I was warmly welcomed by his family and they all seemed to be interested in the Royal Family and London.

They asked me about the Queen and I told them that when we lived in Britain, we visited London several times because Margaret's older sister lived there, but we never saw the Queen! Bruno's wife and her sister longed to return to Poland, and they asked me if we'd be returning to England. At this point I just shrugged and smiled and genuinely didn't know my true answer.

Over the next few days, I began to wonder if we'd made the right decision to emigrate to Australia because if Bruno – who had lived and worked here for about ten years - could end up in such a rough area to live, how could any of us ever afford to buy land, never mind a house? This scenario didn't feature in any of the advertisements nor the promotional material for the £10 Pom scheme!

Back in England it was winter heading into spring. Elsie kept the letters coming from back home and even included interesting clippings from the local newspapers. Around this time, she sent us clippings of photos of heavy snowfall and deep snowdrifts accompanied by descriptions of lots of people who needed rescuing from their homes. The temperatures were well below freezing, so cold that pipes burst and heating systems broke leaving some people living in the cold for a few weeks until they were dug-out of their igloo-like homes. We showed these clippings to our friends on the camp and they were very pleased to see stories about familiar bleak winter weather, although they felt sorry of course for the people back home who were suffering.

Our home city, Hull is in the north of England on the east coast, where strong winds, heavy rain and snow were common, which to us meant a regular winter. I think those of us from parts of the world with four distinct seasons every year felt that the changing seasons were more real than this constant, year-round sunshine. I never realised how much I loved Britain's changing weather and seasons until we came to live in Australia.

Margaret was working most weekends, and on a couple of occasions felt sick and needed to come home, which worried us not only because we didn't know the cause of the sickness, but also because to visit a doctor or the hospital cost money. We joined a health scheme and made weekly payments that would cover most of the costs in the event of illness. Margaret's sickness was becoming more frequent, especially in the morning. Could she be pregnant? We had been trying for a second child for the last nine years. We'd been in Australia for only seven months and it happened, Margaret was pregnant! Maybe it was the effects of all that sunshine, I don't know but we were so happy, I kept saying to Margaret, "let the baby be a girl!" Our friends on camp were very pleased for us, we got together to celebrate with a low-key party.

Margaret was getting on well at work, and she used to tell me about some of the things that happened at the hospital. Many of her stories made me feel uneasy about her safety, but I think my imagination got carried away a bit. Her boss was very kind, supportive and caring and even invited us to his house to meet his family and share a meal. He and his family were Australian and lived in a large house with its own massive swimming pool.

Dale was allowed to mess about in it whenever we visited, which meant he never complained about these outings. Our other Australian friends, Carol and Neville were pleased about our baby news and invited us along to their house for a meal. We were becoming a bit of a celebrity family around camp because a pregnant woman on Graylands was a very rare sight.

The days and weeks were now flying by as we went about our daily routines. This was the time of year when the heat became unbearable because although we were heading into autumn and the daily temperatures were dropping from the summer highs, the humidity was increasing. A shared joke among many of the Poms on site was 'what season is it now?!' 'Summer? Maybe summer? Or it could be summer, no, it's definitely summer!' Even though it was autumn, it felt a lot hotter than an English summer ever did.

I got another NuRoof felting job for a few days down near Albany. I dreaded returning to the smell of the whaling station, but this time I couldn't smell it, I don't know why. NuRoof must have seen me as a senior roofing man by this time because they partnered me up with a new starter. He might have been Italian; I couldn't tell and was happy he spoke good English because it made my life a lot easier. He showed himself to be a good bitumen-felter, but there was something about him that made me feel occasionally uneasy. He was used to working further north in Dampier, about 950 miles (1530 kilometres) north of Perth. I think maybe he was gay because I remember feeling grateful that we had separate hotel rooms - I wasn't bad-looking in those days even if I say so myself!

Our job was on the roof of the pub in a sad little town (more like the size of an English hamlet than a town) just outside Albany. It seemed strange at the time that the religious owners of NuRoof accepted a lot of work from pubs even though they shunned alcohol as much as Alec shunned the tv! In the fierce Australian heat, the bitumen-ed felting didn't last long and regularly needed renewing, and NuRoof seemed to have the monopoly on this type of work. Sometimes we needed to lay down three layers of felt because the sun would burn through one layer in a few weeks or months.

On the approach to the hamlet, we saw many Aboriginal people sprawled about on the dusty roads drinking lager, both men and women alike. My workmate seemed to know all about their lives, he said they had no work and nothing to look forward to and got money for lager by begging. These poor, long-suffering people were a very sad sight to see, you couldn't help but think they got terrible treatment when the White people from the West appeared, and their native habitats were taken away from them. I started to wonder if I was one of those White men. But we'd been invited by the Australian government. I didn't really understand what was going on but I knew it made me feel confused and somehow bad for coming to Australia. I never forgot seeing those poor lost souls lying about in the streets, with nowhere to go and nothing to do except drink lager. What sort of life was that?

Being with my new maybe-Italian workmate, who was very fond of talking, made me think of Margaret's first job in Australia. Before she got the job at the hospital, she worked with an English woman from London called 'Jo' whose husband also worked in the outback. Margaret and Jo got a job in an ice cream factory where most of the workers were Italians. Margaret said that when they were all chatting together the noise level went through the roof. Margaret and Jo couldn't stand it for long and didn't stay beyond a few weeks. They said it was as noisy as a football match on a Saturday afternoon back in England when all the fans were shouting. It was shortly after leaving that Margaret got a job at the local hospital and was much happier.

On one of Margaret's weekends off, we visited the outdoor lido that was a sectioned-off stretch of the Swan River. Health-wise it should never have been allowed to open due to the amount of debris floating about in it. Nevertheless, Dale and me, we went for a swim while Margaret stayed in the shade with a cool drink. There were a few Europeans swimming, we could tell by their accents, but no Australians which perhaps should have set alarm bells ringing. About one week later my ears began aching and then discharging some horrible stinky pus. A visit to the doctors and a few dollars lighter, I was told to stay off work for a week or two due to a bad ear infection. Needless to say, we didn't go swimming in the Swan River again. Thankfully, Dale's ears were fine.

CHAPTER 10

Autumn rolls on and with it comes a scary incident

Many families were moving off the camp and away to other cities: Sidney, Melbourne and others over on the east coast to look for higher paid jobs in better working conditions than I'd found so far working in the outback. The Nissen huts didn't stay empty for long. They were soon occupied by the new immigrant arrivals who turned them into their first homes in their new country.

Out-of-the-blue, Sam called one evening to ask if I wanted to go with him to work on a site up north a few miles from Port Hedland. This was about a 1000-mile (1600-kilometre) drive from Graylands. Sam and family would take their caravan and I would drive a ute to carry a load of galvanized aluminium sheets and other roofing materials. There were other workers on site and accommodation for us. I would need to be away from Margaret and Dale for a few weeks, which worried me, but our friends on Graylands said they would keep an eye on them and they'd be fine.

I arranged with a bank in Perth for all my wages to be paid directly into a bank account. Sam was sub-contracting this job again from NuRoof, and he arranged all of the finances with the company as he had done previously. I was very sad to be leaving Margaret and Dale. I didn't linger too long before waving them goodbye, as I set-off to meet Sam and family for our long drive north.

I arrived early at Sam's house and away we all went. We knew we'd be driving for at least a day and a half and maybe longer, which I thought would be no problem because Sam's ute was air-conditioned. We began near the coast and headed inland and northeast for about 700 miles (1130 kilometres) to a town called Newman, for the first overnight stop. Sam booked me into a hotel for that night, he and his family slept in their caravan.

On the second day, we began to drive north up to Port Hedland. The drive became a nightmare when we left behind the tarmac roads and had to make our way on dusty tracks. Good old Sam was as prepared as ever and gave me a pair of driving goggles and a mask to protect me from the sandy, thick dust thrown up by our vehicles. Being so far inland meant no sea breeze to cool the air. Instead, it was unchangingly hot and opening the window wasn't an option because that would let in even more thick, brown dust than found its way in through the dashboard's vents. At times, the visibility was so poor Sam couldn't see me following him, and I could only just make out the lights of their caravan. Our speeds slowed to a crawl and the drive across this barren scrubland seemed endless.

Eventually, we reached smoother and less dusty tracks and could see some of the surrounding terrain; we passed many occupied Aborigine hamlets, patches of tough-looking vegetation and one or two families of three or four kangaroos – the first I'd seen since arriving in Australia! Blimey, could they hop - covering about 20 feet (six metres) in one go! In the distance we saw gangs of men working on the railway lines, which explained the improvement in the road tracks. The rail company was responsible for ensuring its massive trucks carrying heavy sleepers and tracks could safely reach the worksites deep in the outback. Somehow, they had flattened and compressed the dust into solid road surfaces, maybe by the sheer weight of the vehicles themselves.

Sam's family were used to these conditions having previously travelled to various jobs in the caravan, although this trip was the furthest they'd yet travelled. They were well-prepared for the long journey carrying plenty of water and supplies in their caravan. Maureen had packed a pile of books and games to keep herself and the two girls occupied and distracted, while Sam concentrated on driving and towing the caravan. We had made such slow progress that we spent a second night on the road, this time all of us shared the caravan.

After two days and two nights our destination was in sight and we'd finally got through this gruelling experience. I was glad when, somewhere along the way, we came across a group of truckers who directed us to the safest tracks and roads. It was pretty obvious that you needed to respect the land and conditions over here and be prepared for survival when travelling across this country through the barren outback. Most of the time, the workers heading for Port Hedland covered the distance we'd travelled from Perth by light aircraft, and although it was probably safer it would have been a less memorable journey.

Sam estimated the job would take us about three weeks, which meant three weeks working with big black swarms of angry flies buzzing around our heads. We were lucky to spot several snakes before accidentally startling them, instead, we managed to keep out of their way. Our English grass snakes seemed almost friendly compared to these potential killers! Hazards from the local wildlife were par for the course by now.

We'd brought along some materials and sheeting, but we needed more and needed to wait half a day for the trucks transporting the roofing sheets from Port Hedland to deliver their load to us. We spent the time watching the workers using ladders and ropes to erect the scaffold around the skeleton of the building we would clad. Even with the scaffold, I couldn't work out how we'd get to the top. This structure was a lot taller than the one we'd worked on down in Albany.

"Don't worry Yorkie, stick with me and we'll soon be up there, getting the job done and on our way back to Perth." I was none-the-wiser but trusted him. When the scaffolders had finished, somehow Sam got himself up to the top of the skeleton. Once there, he rigged-up pulleys and a bosun's chair, (a few planks of wood tied together with ropes to make a platform) and my job was to load the aluminium sheets onto the chair and hoist them up towards Sam who was pulling from the top of the building. I didn't mind that part of the job but I was worried about climbing from the top of the scaffolding across the gap up to the roof girders, and it took all my mental effort to not think about falling through the gap and hitting the ground almost 90 feet (about 27 metres) below.

Sam guided me up to the roof girders and showed me how to safely navigate the gap, and there I was at the very top, I'd done it! That's when it was time for the work to begin. Sam lined up the galvanized sheets across the girders and my job was to screw them down. It didn't take me long to get used to working up high and I began to feel I was on top of the world ('Ma!'), albeit a scorched and parched one. Thankfully, Sam had brought us each a pair of sunshield goggles to reduce the sun's glare off the shiny aluminium sheeting, but at times it was still difficult to see where to drill.

Skeleton warehouse and structures at the worksite; me on top of the world!

"Look to your right!" Sam shouted across to me. When I did, I saw a lake of shimmering water that I hadn't noticed before.

"It's not what you think, Yorkie, it's a mirage." It happens when conditions are right for the sun to reflect off the sand and dust, bringing to life a blue lagoon. It was truly amazing, and I found it hard to believe it wasn't a lake.

We worked for a couple of hours then took a break, climbing down under the sheets onto the girders where we swigged the water and ate the sandwiches that Maureen had prepared and packed for us. Sitting there on the girder, legs swinging with about 80 feet (about 24 metres) of thick, stale, sun-soaked air between us and the ground, drinking refreshing, cool water and eating fresh sandwiches made me feel downright scared and happy at the same time. This was pretty much how I felt most of the time I lived in Australia.

Sam sensed that I wasn't feeling great about our working conditions, so he made a makeshift seat from a couple of planks left behind by the scaffolders and tied it securely to the girders. Phew! I felt a lot safer sitting on that. He told me that when we had a few more sheets pinned down I'd begin to feel a lot better about working up so high. All I could do was trust the man who sang, 'Maybe it's because I'm a Londoner' while carrying two timber planks over his shoulders along 12-inch-wide girders, 80 feet (24 metres) above the ground.

"Well Yorkie," he said, smiling and winking at me, "the first day is always the worst! Let's get on and beat the currant bun!" That first day, Sam worked about six feet (two metres) away from me and didn't stop talking about his home city, London. Of course, he knew what he was doing and the distraction work; by the end of that first day, I was getting into the swing of things and gradually losing my fear of heights. We ended the day back in the caravan with all five of us enjoying a lovely meal, thanks to Maureen.

The worksite had temporary accommodation and an office with a telephone to coordinate the deliveries of trucked materials from Port Hedland. Judging by appearances and from overheard snippets of conversations in different languages, the worksite was populated with workers from across the world. The office staff were all white Australians, but none of the manual workers were. At night I stayed in the Graylands-like accommodation in the Nissen huts but there was no privacy at all. The showering and shaving facilities were shared by everyone, so I didn't do either for a while! I must have looked a right scruffy sight and stank too, but so did everyone in those conditions.

After bidding them 'goodnight' and leaving Sam and family in their caravan, I began to feel very lonely and longed for Margaret and Dale. In those moments they might as well have been living on another planet, they felt that far away from me.

With each passing day we saw the results of our efforts and eventually the roof was finished. We then began to work our way down the building fixing the aluminium sheets to its sides from the top to the bottom. We worked non-stop until the second Saturday into our three-week stay when Sam said it was time to take a break. Maureen had taken the girls into Port Hedland and we took off into the scrub a couple of miles from camp. Sam brought along an air rifle, which I didn't know he carried. He said it was 'for protection when working in the outback'.

We took a few grogs with us and found a circle of dead bush trees and shot at their branches to break them off using as few pellets as possible. It was good fun and the first time I'd ever done anything like that. We moved a bit further into the scrub and bet on who could shoot down the most twigs, which cost me a hard-earned five-dollar bill. I didn't mind losing it to Sam, we were having a good time. When we eventually got back to the ute, there was a group of four or five massive emus close by.

Sam whispered, "Yorkie, walk slowly and quietly back to the ute and don't startle the buggers, 'cos if you do and they charge at us, we need to start praying!" When we got back to the ute, Sam jumped into the driving seat and reversed into our pellet-shooting area. If the emu-gang changed their minds and began to charge, at least we would have some distance between us to lessen their impact. I don't think I was scared, it was all happening too fast to feel anything but excitement at this new adventure, even though we were in real danger.

By the time we reversed, the emus had become interested in us and started trotting after the ute, picking-up speed very quickly. Quick-as-a-flash, Sam opened his door, one hand on the driving wheel. With the other hand he shot repeatedly at the ground just in front of the emus, kicking-up enough dust to make them turn around and run in the opposite direction, pelting along even faster than when they were chasing us. I reckon they got up to about 25 miles per hour (40 kilometres per hour). They really were big buggers too, standing at about six feet (two metres) tall! Later, Sam said the group could easily have tipped over the ute with us inside, and I believed him.

Back at Sam's caravan we got a warm welcome home as usual, which left me with a sharp pang as I realised how much I was missing Margaret and Dale, and even the baby that wasn't yet born. Once again, I questioned whether this sort of life was what I really wanted for my family; was life in Australia always going to be like this – working away to earn enough money to get by? On the other hand, we were having the adventure of a lifetime, or at least I was. That night, Maureen and the girls sat and listened to Sam and me tell them about our day's close encounter with the emus. Maureen wasn't too happy about the rifle but agreed that it seemed to be a good idea to have one to hand in the outback.

Spending so much time with Sam and his family was great but I often felt I was getting in their way, not because they ever said as much nor did anything to make me feel that, I think I felt that because I wanted my own family around me. I wrote to Margaret often, and when Maureen drove to Port Hedland for supplies, she dropped off my letters for delivery by the light aircraft that brought in the mail and more new workers, and returned to Perth with those that were homeward bound.

Every evening saw a hive of activity at the worksite different to daytime when many of the men stopped working and started to gamble. They placed bets on the Two-up game that involved flicking two cent coins into the air and placing a bet on the face they'd land on – it was the Aussie version of 'Heads or Tails'. Hundreds of dollars were won and lost on pay day, with some fellas losing their entire wages in one night to Two-up and grog. The grog was one of the essentials brought onto site along with the roofing materials from Port Hedland, and it was kept cool by an on-site generator. There'd probably have been a walk-out if the grog ever ran out.

By now, I was getting used to working at these heights, which were decreasing as we made our way around and down the sides of the building. The days fell into a regular pattern with nothing of note happening until one day when Sam appeared from his caravan looking a bit 'off' and out-of-sorts, although he didn't say why and I didn't ask. Anyway, we started on our day's work with each of us standing either side on the bosun's chair along with the aluminium sheeting, the two of us working the pulley ropes to hoist ourselves and the sheeting upwards.

When we first started on this job, Sam had stressed that the ties on the bosun's chair needed checking and securing every morning, and we'd both got into that routine. On this particular day, we were about 30 feet (nine metres) above the ground when Sam screamed. I turned toward him and saw the rope securing his side of the chair had slipped making it tilt, tipping Sam out. As he fell, he grabbed onto the bottom of the chair and was left dangling mid-air. By this time my side became unstable too because the chair was now unbalanced. I was glad I had double-checked the ties to the sheeting else they would have slid out of the chair and hit Sam on their way down. By now my heart was thumping away in my chest.

"Sam, hold on you Cockney bugger!" I shouted, and slowly, slowly unwound my side of the rope to lower us to the ground. Eventually - it must have seemed forever to Sam - we were low enough for him to jump down safely. How the hell he had the strength to hang on like that, I don't know but thank the Big Almighty he did.

By the time we reached the ground a gang of workers had come over to check if we were okay. We were both alive, but not really okay. We were shaken-up and decided to knock-off work for the day. We trudged back to Sam's caravan and told Maureen about the accident. She cried and let loose about not wanting to be over here in this country any longer and how she wanted to go back home to England. At this point I left them to carry on and returned to the worksite to check the ropes. By the look of Sam's rope and how poorly it was secured, I was right about him being out-of-sorts. Usually, he checked mine as well as his own, so whatever he'd been upset about must have been big for this lapse in his routine. I didn't feel right for the rest of the day and somehow occupied myself before checking in on them all later on.

The following day we carried on working as if nothing had happened, Sam didn't talk about the previous day's incident, but he did start talking fondly about his younger brother. One day, they were walking to the local shop as they usually did, when suddenly his brother ran across the road without looking, straight into a car that killed him outright. I think Sam's sadness was increased by his feelings of guilt at being the older, responsible brother who 'should' have kept his little brother safe. I wondered if perhaps he'd taken me under his wing because I reminded him of his brother. I couldn't go back to Sam's caravan that evening, there were too many emotions in the air, and I felt too sad to spend more time with him.

The next day he was back to his usual self and told me that lately he and Maureen had been shouting at each other a lot, which of course upset the girls. The nomadic working lifestyle was taking its toll and I wondered if this would be me and my family's fate too if we stayed in this country. I was now feeling really down and pined for home back at Graylands with Margaret and Dale. Big Bill's words came to mind: 'This country and this heat drive everyone mad in the end!' and I wondered, if you didn't go mad did you become sad instead?

I breathed a massive sigh of relief when the final row of aluminium sheeting was checked and signed-off by one of the worksite office staff. Sam decided we should spend one last night on camp before driving over to Port Hedland for supplies. We were going to drive back to Perth along the coast road, where we'd find cooler air and could bathe and swim in the Indian Ocean. The release of tension in all of us was clear to see as we tucked into another of Maureen's lovely meals, this time celebrating the completion of a job well done. I was very happy thinking I'd soon be back with Margaret and Dale. The following day we did a final check of the vehicles and Sam shook my hand.

"What's this all about?" I asked.

"You know, Yorkie!" He replied with a wink, "you've got a lot of courage and got through it all like a true Cockney!"

"Piss off, you Cockney bugger – like a true Yorkie you mean!" I grinned.

"Whatever, you've had a taste of real sheeting work!" Once again, this was getting a bit too much for me, I knew he was really talking about the bosun's chair and I began to fill-up and turned away from him. We never talked about it again. Sam and family waited for me while I took one last look around, wondering if I'd ever return to this site.

Later that day we arrived at the town of Port Hedland and stocked-up on essentials plus a few gifts, followed by a meal in a café.

Sam asked, "Will you come and work with me again then, Yorkie?"

I shrugged, "Maybe? I'm not a green Pom any more am I, so maybe I will!" The five of us shared a chuckle and I got a sense that we also shared the feeling of being pioneers from a faraway land, trying to survive in our new hostile home. One hundred miles (160 kilometres) later we'd parked-up and were watching the sun setting over the Indian Ocean. That night I slept in the ute - it was either that or on the ground under the stars, and I didn't fancy becoming an overnight snack for scorpions, poison spiders and snakes.

The next day we were up early; Maureen made a lovely breakfast of eggs and toast, before we set-off on our long drive back to civilization. The coast route was a lot cooler than our inland dusty trek. After about five hours of driving, we pulled into a garage to fill-up the ute and the jerry cans with fuel, restock our water supplies, stretch our bodies and eat.

The driving condition of the roads was improving although at times there were clouds of dust, perhaps you couldn't escape dust over here. Now and then I spotted a kangaroo or two hopping along, and a few dead ones sprawled across the road. At one point we had to stop and drag a dead 'roo off the road and on to the nearby scrub. There were more truckers passing us the closer we got to Perth. They were heading in the opposite direction, on their way to Port Hedland or further still to Darwin. They always flashed the 'hello' signal with their headlights adding a few toots from their horns, and we flashed our lights in return. I was really enjoying this drive and thought what an adventure it must have been for Sam and Maureen's two daughters, but perhaps they were bored stiff!

I began to notice new houses being built by the coast and dreaded to think how much they cost. I also noticed more road signs appearing, and realised they were few and far between the further you got from a big city. After one more overnight stop our journey came to an end and Sam suggested that when we reached Perth we would split, me to Graylands, Sam and family back to their home. I couldn't wait to get back to hut 129D.

When I did finally walk through the door of our Nissen hut, Margaret was surprised to see me. Since leaving nearly three weeks ago there had been no communication between us at all except for my letters, and the last time I wrote I didn't know when we'd finish the job and get back to Perth. Margaret's first words to me when I walked through the door of our hut made me smile.

"Well, get yourself over to the wash house then and have a good wash - you stink!" I had to smile, that was Margaret all right! I noticed she was looking tired and her ankles were swollen. Later she said her boss had given her some lighter jobs around the hospital. Dale was nowhere to be seen, he was out and about as usual on his own adventures. When he did return, he said a bird flew by and pecked his head, but he didn't know what type of bird it was.

"Here's the cut to prove it, dad," he said scraping his hair back proudly showing me the gash. Luckily, he didn't need to go to the hospital that time!

CHAPTER 11

Winter (June to August), we shell out on some furniture, and I go to work at a brewery

During the week Dale walked to a school with a couple of friends from the camp. He fitted in well at the school making more friends there, although he once told me there was a lot of name-calling because they were the kids living on the Migrant Camp. Kids will be kids!

Dale told me they were all given a tree to plant along the sandbank close to school, to stop it from eroding, and they had to write their name on a label and attach it to the tree. I don't suppose Dale's tree, nor any of them are still there. Sometimes, when Margaret and I were out at work, Dale had to let himself back into the hut when he got home from school, so we gave him his own key tying it to a piece of string around his neck. We also told him to make sure he took his knife, fork and spoon to the canteen at mealtimes if we weren't going to be back in time to eat as a family. Most of the time he remembered, or at least told us he had.

Sam and family paid us a visit a few times and we all headed down to the beach. I decided to have a couple of weeks off, and Sam lent us his ute until I got another job with NuRoof and the use of one of their utes. On one of Margaret's weekends off we went to Perth city to look for a small table for our home. Walking around the shopping area (no window-cleaner in sight!) and peering in the windows, we saw an advert for a small table for sale. The person selling it lived in a suburb close to Graylands called Subiaco. We found a phone box and arranged to go round and view the table straight away.

The seller was an Aussie bloke who welcomed us into his home and showed us his collection of shells from some islands where he lived or worked in his younger days. There were some real 'beauts', lovely shapes, colours and shell-types: deep water, sun and shore. Margaret was fascinated by them, which encouraged the bloke to show us more and more shells. I think he must have been lonely and appreciated the company because he said he hardly ever saw anyone where he lived, everyone stayed indoors to keep cool when they weren't at work.

Sam looking like the Cat Who Got the Cream lazing between his wife, Maureen and Margaret (holding on to her sunhat)

We bought the table and as we were leaving, he gave us a bag and told Margaret to pick a few shells to take away with us. She chose a few, I am looking at them now as I write this, fifty plus years later. Seeing the table-seller's shells made me think that the next time I worked away, I would look for interesting objects to remind me of places I'd been, and it's a habit I still have today. What a great day that was! It was one of the few times, I felt we were welcome in Australia, all thanks to one man and his shells! We finished the day with some delicious Italian ice cream bought from a small shop near the train station.

A couple of days later there was a message waiting for me at Graylands' office about some new work with NuRoof. I went and found out it was all local work, felting the roofs of houses in the Perth suburbs, plus a job felting the roof of the Swan River Brewery. NuRoof gave me the use of a work ute, but shortly after getting it home it refused to start, so the firm arranged for it to be towed to their regular garage. I was annoyed because that brought an end to our spontaneous weekend family outings, and once again I was on the train every morning and night travelling backwards and forwards to Perth. The novelty of it had worn off by now because by the time I got home it was dark; at that time of year that was around five o'clock.

I had too much time to think when travelling by train and spent a lot of time wondering if all this effort was worth it. Sometimes, I didn't want to start work the next day. I did begin to form one idea that cheered me up and my mood lifted further when one day Sam rolled up at Graylands and said there was another job in the pipeline, probably in a few weeks. It was a lot nearer Perth, sheeting a new works storage building and would take us one week at the most. He wouldn't take his family this time, it would just be the two of us.

"Are you interested, Yorkie?" he asked. He would sort out all the sub-contracting paperwork with NuRoof.

"Count me in Cockney!" I replied without hesitating.

I spent the next week or so working locally and then it was time to start on the Swan Brewery job. By now the temperature was dropping but the humidity was increasing. Bruno and me, we were told to go sort out the brewery because the owners weren't happy with the work that another company had done. We could see why when we inspected the roof. We ordered some new rolls of felt, but before we could lay these, everything had to be stripped clean and the job started from scratch. This meant the job was going to take longer than everyone first thought. I didn't mind at all because it was nice and cool thanks to the overall drop in temperature and also the brewery was situated on the riverbank. I was happy because the views along the river of all the seacraft coming and going on the choppy water were brilliant, and Bruno was a great worker and I enjoyed his company.

We were very lucky because there was already a crane on site that had been used to hoist up onto the roof the gas bottles, barrels of bitumen and all the work tools we needed. This gear was either left by the previous workers or arranged to be there ready for us to begin. Neither of us were in a rush and we took our time on the job.

While we waited for the bitumen to heat up, we paid a visit to see what was inside the factory where all the brewery workers were. Phew! The smell of malt and other ingredients it took to make the local grog was overpowering, and combined with the heat sent us rushing back towards the indoor stairs to the roof. Before we could get back, though, there was a loud hooting sound. At one end of the factory two big doors opened and workers from all directions began to form a line that stretched from one end of the factory to the other. Through the opened doors, we saw a few barrels of grog and lots of glasses placed out on a long table. The line of men filed past the table and were handed a tot of grog which they promptly glugged down, then they rejoined the end of the line for another tot. It was total mayhem with workers running to join the line.

One worker rushed past us. "Come on lads don't miss your turn!" he said, so of course we just followed and joined the long queue. We just reached the grog and got a taste when once again the hooter sounded and the doors were closed, signalling it was time for everyone to go back to their jobs. We reckoned this happened about three or four times a day judging by the number of hooter-blasts we counted.

We went back up to the roof to continue working.

I said to Bruno, "I thought you didn't drink?" A broad smile spread across his face.

"What I do down there in that line? I must drink, no? But I not go down again!" Before we had finished for the day the hooter sounded a few more blasts and we both ignored it and carried on working.

Felting that brewery roof was a pleasure and was easy work compared to what I usually did. Even though we stretched it out for as long as possible, within about ten days it came to an end. An inspector from NuRoof was sent to check our work and sign it off, and all was going well until the brewery hooter blasted.

Swan River Brewery at night (taken from a greetings card made by 'Rogerson Card')

"What's that?" he asked, "do we need to evacuate the building?" Bruno and I looked over at each other, shook our heads and kept quiet. By this time the inspector was heading down into the brewery, which meant he would have to walk down the brewery stairs, straight into the line of workers queueing up for their grog. Within a few minutes the inspector was back on the roof babbling about 'evil alcohol' with a scared and angry look on his face.

Then he turned to me. "Go and see if they've all gone back to work down there!" Only then would he leave. When he had, Bruno and me, we sat in the shade for the rest of the afternoon, sharing a good laugh and a natter. We agreed that NuRoof's religion was a bit difficult to understand! Didn't they know the job was felting a *brewery* roof? The following day was another easy one spent waiting for a crane driver to appear to help us get the tools and work gear down off the roof. Then it was all over and finished and we were wondering where our next job would take us. I hoped Sam would call about the job he'd mentioned, but he didn't and must have been working away again.

CHAPTER 12

Wintery wanderings and a weak leg

Graylands had its own noticeboard where people pinned notes about all sorts of different things, some of them jobs, some of them things for sale and some of them about trips out. I spotted one about a trip to some waterfalls advertised by a private coach company, a local firm out of Perth, and as luck would have it the day trip fell on Margaret's weekend off. I registered our names at the office and when the day came the three of us waited on site with other Graylands day-trippers for the coach to come and pick us up. We climbed aboard, paid our fares, found some free seats and sat back to enjoy the day.

We drove south from Perth through Fremantle then further on down the coast. When we reached the 'waterfalls' I had to laugh because they were more like a 'water-trickle'. I had been picturing something like High Force in the Yorkshire Dales – that was my idea of a waterfall! All that anticipation of the trip and the wonders we might see ended in an anti-climax. I felt boosted though when Margaret said her workmate Carol was very impressed that we visited as many places as we could. She said they had not ventured very far and she called us an 'Adventurous Family' which made me feel very proud.

New families continued to arrive on Graylands, while others left. There was a family from Lincolnshire who had become our friends, and they were approaching their two-year time limit at Graylands. They told us that six months ago they booked spaces for them all on the liner back to England. This wasn't a surprise because they had said many times that Australia wasn't for them. They were sick of the terrible working conditions and felt the Brits weren't at all welcomed by the Australians. Their only friends were expat Poms on Graylands. Even though they said they could afford to buy some land and get on the housing ladder, they wanted to return to Britain.

When the time came, we went with them down to the port at Fremantle to wave them off. What an emotional goodbye that was, with lots of hugging and tears that didn't only fall from the lasses' eyes! I don't know where they got them from, but they were waving Union Jack flags from onboard the liner. We stood and watched the majestic ship slowly manoeuvre its way out of Fremantle Port to begin its long journey across the Indian Ocean, carrying hundreds of ex-immigrants back to their own homelands.

We lost touch with the Lincolnshire family, but I often thought of them and wondered how their lives changed over the passing years. I understood how they felt about Australia and why they were returning to Britain, but a part of me felt let down – we'd been in this life together and that gave all of us immigrant Poms some strength. Every family we had come to know that went home, left us feeling weaker and less determined to stay.

On the way back to the ute my left lower leg folded-up and totally gave way, I could only walk on tiptoes. Bloody hell, the pain was terrible! I don't know how I managed it, but I drove us home from Fremantle, got myself to the bed and laid down. I was told I had torn my hamstring and a couple of ligaments and needed to rest for at least a week. Someone from NuRoof paid a visit and arranged a pickup for the ute while I was unable to work.

On top of the pain in my leg I was scared about what might happen if this was a long-term injury. I was starting to panic and tried to hide it from Margaret, not wanting to worry her and Dale. My thoughts were racing all over the place: what happens now that I am laid-up like this with no family around to help? And we've got a baby on the way, and a lot of the Grayland Poms who would help if needed, were moving away to other states or seemed to vanish into thin air. (They were of course heading home on the ocean liners, but I wasn't very rational at this point).

I felt that our life in Australia was turning into dust – the same thick choking dust I drove through in the outback. Maybe that's why the country was so dusty - it was the broken dreams of all the people who had come here full of hope and adventure, only to be crushed by this damn place. I was panicking and anxious. Fortunately, the initial shock of the injury gradually wore off. I calmed down and after a few days of bed rest my leg was already feeling stronger, and with it my sense of hope and confidence that we would be okay.

The idea I'd first thought of a few weeks ago when travelling to Perth and back on the train, reappeared: from now on we needed to try and save as much money as we could to send back to a building society account back in England. Margaret agreed, and being a Yorkie family meant there was only one savings society we could choose, and that was the Halifax Building Society.

I wanted to make sure we had enough savings to buy our passage back to Britain if we decided to return. Margaret was less keen to leave because she wanted to see more of Australia, but we couldn't do that and save at the same time. Also, when our two years at Graylands were up, we would need to spend money moving away; either as money upfront for rent on a house, or as a down payment on a caravan to travel across the country to seek our fortune further east.

We also discussed what might happen if we became ill, because although we paid into a scheme to cover visits to the doctor, medical treatments and any stays in hospital, what would happen if we were driving around in the outback and became ill? There would be no neighbours and no family to help us.

It became obvious the Immigration Authorities wanted us to move off the Graylands camp, when they began to regularly send us information and brochures about new building projects springing up in the suburbs of Perth. They even arranged free transport to visit the building sites. I don't know how many Poms took up their offer. We didn't because we'd already seen how much some of these new builds cost, and they were way out of our reach. Instead of enticing us to stay, these brochures made us talk about saving-up and discussing what our long-term plans might be. They mostly involved returning home to Britain. When my leg healed and I could walk properly again, we visited a travel agent in Perth for some advice about the fares of passage on a liner back to England.

CHAPTER 13

Winter continues, wet weather and I W.A.C.A. scorpion or two

The days were passing by quickly. Margaret's baby bump was beginning to show and she was feeling tired a lot of the time. I was worried that she would feel worse when winter ended, and the temperature began to rise in spring. One evening, we were surprised by a clattering sound on the roof of our hut, it took us a few seconds before we recognised it as raindrops. We opened the door and found lots of our neighbours already outside enjoying the feeling of rain on their skin, some of them started whooping and cheering then somebody started to clap and we all joined in. A year ago, I was moaning about how much rain there was in Hull, and here I was happy to get soaking wet! We were all happy to get some respite from the heat – our metal huts were almost as hot at night as they were during the day, even in winter.

Now that my leg was fully healed, I was back working for NuRoof again and about to start a job at one of the best places a big cricket fan like me could be: the Western Australia Cricket Association (W.A.C.A.) ground in Perth city. I had loved cricket from boyhood and in my schooldays played in the wicket keeper's position. Mr Codd (my sports teacher) was impressed with my ability to judge the ball's line of flight as it came hurtling towards the batter. I never would have believed I'd visit the W.A.C.A. ground, one of the best in the world, never mind actually work on it!

Bruno was in charge of a small gang of four of us, all of them Polish except me. Our job was to lay and roll a couple of 22 yards (20 metres) long practice pitches. I was assigned to use a small roller to flatten the pitches and make sure they were completely level. First though, we dug out the rectangles for the pitches, rolled the ground then filled it with hardcore; next came a layer of bitumen poured on top, followed by layers of felt making a total thickness of about 18 inches (46 centimetres).

That job was a total pleasure for me. I felt so proud to be working on this cricket ground that was known across the world, and where our very own English lads played. Sometimes, I swear I could hear the crowd shouting England on in the Ashes Series. I knew this would become a treasured memory and I hope it stays with me for the rest of my life.

The work was going well and passed the inspector's daily checks of pitch length and depth. One day there was a thunderstorm causing us to knock-off until it passed. Within a few minutes of the rain stopping everything was dry again. This happened so frequently it delayed our progress. NuRoof wasn't very happy when we told them the job would take about a week, but they had to accept that's how long it takes to do a good job. I think their religion was okay with cricket.

On about the fourth day, I was pitch-rolling happily along when suddenly there was a shout from the other end of the pitch. I ran over and saw a cluster of scorpions, and one of the workers beating them over and over again in blind panic. This made the situation worse because the scorpions scuttled around in all directions. Bruno appeared with a gas burner and burnt as many scorpions as he could. Then the groundsman came over with a club official and told us the only way to get rid of these stingers for good was to dig down, find their nest, drench it in flammable liquid and set fire to the whole lot. He told us the same thing had happened before around the edges of the ground, and that was the only way to get rid of them.

We reckoned that the vibrations from the roller had disturbed the scorpions and caused them to surface. We started digging and after only a few inches we found the nest overflowing with them; It made my skin crawl to see their pincers nipping this way and that. We decided to dig around the hole making it bigger and then poured in some kerosene, ignited it with the burner and 'vwhoomp!' up it went in flames. Ugh! The smell was overpowering, after the fire died down all that was left was a lump of black stuff that looked like melted tar. We didn't come across any more scorpions after that.

A few days later the job was finished, checked and passed with flying colours and we spent an easy last day slowly traipsing backwards and forwards in between the shower spells, pushing a wheelbarrow carrying our work gear back to the ute. We always took bottles of water on jobs with us and if there was any running water on site, we used to stick our hands and heads in it to cool off. I did that one last time at the W.A.C.A. and took a final look around before pelting down the pitch and shouting 'Howzat!' as I bowled an overarm googly.

CHAPTER 14

There's gold in them thar fields, and a site for a sore eye

After a few more local jobs with NuRoof, Sam and family appeared again about the job he'd mentioned a few weeks ago. Sam's daughters were pleased to see Dale and off the three of them went to play outside. Sam reminded me that the job he mentioned before was in the outback but only a few hours outside Perth, we would be working with galvanized sheeting, and it would take us between one and two weeks. I know I had agreed to do it, but I had mixed feelings: happy to work with Sam, sad to leave Margaret and Dale for over a week, but happy to think of the dollars we would send to our savings account. Margaret wasn't happy at all, but agreed it was one of the only ways we could save enough money to buy our tickets back home to Old Blighty, if that's what we eventually decided to do.

I said to Sam, "I hope the job isn't up too high this time!"

"No way," he replied with a glint in his eyes. About a week later he appeared early in his ute. I loaded my small bag containing a few shirts, shorts and basic toiletries in the back, alongside the bag of provisions Sam had packed for our 'short' six- or seven-hour drive.

We left Perth on solid, tarmacked roads - soon leaving them behind as we drove further into the outback on dusty tracks. Sam said they were probably the original tracks made by Aboriginal people, and later used by White settlers making their way across Australia. We made a few stops along the way, one of them to look at some gum trees that had no leaves at all, maybe due to the time of year. We spotted some markings on a few of the trees that Sam recognised as Aboriginal family tribal markings. They meant this was their area, there was a settlement nearby, and other tribal families weren't allowed to go there. I looked closer at the tree and saw the markings had been intricately carved and looked like they were smeared with blood.

Sam said we were probably being watched – we couldn't see anybody, but from his experience he knew that they knew we were there. I was getting a little bit afraid, which increased when the sound of chanting started-up, along with a breeze that suddenly blew up from nowhere. With that, we scarpered back to the ute and I almost prayed the engine would start, I wanted to be out of there – fast! When Sam told me the Aboriginal people had been driven away from a lot of their land by the first White Australian settlers, I felt sorry and thought back to the sight of Aboriginal men and women lying about in the streets drinking lager down near Albany. What would I do in their situation? Impossible to know.

Eventually, we reached our destination and thankfully, it looked a lot more promising than the site near Port Hedland. In fact, it looked like a small town under construction; even the workers' facilities looked better with an actual, proper block of showers. We booked in at the hotel and finished off the day with a few grogs in the bar. We laughed about how the bar was probably the first building in town to be erected!

The next day we went down to the worksite. I was relieved to find that this time, the roofing work would be only about 30 feet (nine metres) above the ground. All the materials had already been delivered and were ready for us to make a start. The first thing we did was work out where to begin, then we made sure the pulley and ropes to lift-up the roofing sheets were safe and securely tied and fixed.

Next, Sam climbed up the skeleton structure to the top. I stayed at the bottom and together we began to heft the galvanized sheets of metal up onto the roof; one-by-one we pulled them up to the top and screwed them onto the roof girders. They were the lightest we had handled so far. The downside of the sheets was that they were very shiny and bright, and acted like giant mirrors reflecting the sunlight back into our eyes. The goggles Sam brought weren't good enough to protect our eyes from this glare when the sun was strongest, which meant we had to knock-off for a couple of hours until the sun was shining from a different direction. We also had to finish working by late afternoon because the daylight soon disappeared, and darkness descended by about five o'clock at this time of year. The darkness of the outback was relieved by starlight and moonlight.

We spent some of the evening time exploring the area, and realised this was a new town in the making. There was a long way to go before it would be an inhabited and fully functioning town. It was an interesting worksite because there was a lot going on, with many different types of workers: construction, roadbuilders, truckers driving the heavy loads of materials onto site, water-tank drivers, and so on. There were even a couple of small shacks that had been turned into food stores. This site was much better equipped for us workers than any of my previous jobs in the outback, and I felt excited to be there and to be part of building a new town.

Our work was progressing slowly because, although the sheets were a lot lighter than even Sam had worked with, we had to be careful handling them. They got very hot very quickly and with them being so thin, they could easily cut through bare skin. We had to wear thick gloves to handle them, which wasn't easy because the thickness of the gloves made bending the fingers to get a grip difficult. We also wore knee pads to protect our knees – this job needed a lot of kneeling – but they made moving about on the roof awkward.

A few days into the job we heard some talk about gold being found a few miles from the worksite. I don't know how but the news travelled fast and within a few hours we saw hundreds of vehicles, including utes, towing caravans trundling past the worksite. This 'gold-rush' continued through the night judging by the constant din of the vehicle engines, the dust they churned-up and the shouts of 'Gold! Gold!' Back at the hotel, we were told this happened a couple of times a year but that no-one had recently found a decent-sized nugget that they could retire on.

Everyone was heading to a site that was established as a gold mine back in the 1800s, where some small gold finds were still being discovered. When a miner found a fragment that was a bit bigger than the usual pieces, word soon spread that some larger nuggets had made their way to the surface, and hundreds of hopeful miners appeared with their pickaxes and shovels in search of the 'big one'.

Sam and I talked about going out there to see the place for ourselves; we might get lucky and find a big gold nugget! We knocked-off the job early the next day and drove for about an hour out to the goldfields. What a surprising sight it was, hundreds of people swinging pickaxes, tents rigged-up and even a grog wagon had made its way there. The dust was thick and choking, but through it the search for gold continued. Some lads were pegging out some land and claiming that as their area. We found out that eventually they would need to pay to register their land-claim with the Western Australian Government to make it legal.

We heard that somewhere around 1910 to 1920 an old-timer who lived in the outback and was friendly with the local Aborigine tribe, found a glittering and golden coloured rock in this area that turned out to be the biggest gold nugget ever found. When news got around, hopeful goldminers came to these new goldfields to try their luck and the town called Coolgardie grew-up around them. The gold mine is still active to this day and owned by a single company. When Sam and I were there, it was a free-for-all, every-man-for-himself kind of place.

We kept away from everybody, heads down and eyes on the ground searching for some glittering rocks, when suddenly I saw some small pieces shining back up at me. They were telling me to take them back to Old Blighty. I picked them up.

"What have you got there, Yorkie?"

I didn't want to share so I tried to play it cool and replied, "I'm keeping these, Cockney lad!" He grinned and said, "Ok, it's like that is it – the same goes when I find the big 'un!"

I grinned back at him and opened my hand.

"You can keep them Yorkie, it's fool's gold you've found!"

"Sounds right!' I said, but I didn't mind that it wasn't real gold. Like the Aussie man and his shells, I knew I was collecting precious memories, and in this case the memories were golden.

Back at the worksite we were getting used to handling the sheeting, and we adjusted our working hours to avoid the worst of the sun's glare off the aluminium. At night, the sounds of partying and singing drifted over from the goldfields. The hotel owner told us the miners worked at night wearing headlamps because that's when the gold stood out best, shining its brightest reflecting in the lights from the lamps. He was happy there was a lot going on over there because he took the opportunity to send a couple of utes filled with barrels of grog. Sam and me, we went back a week or so after our first visit and were amazed at the changes. There were some huge holes in the ground, a large tent where the finds could be weighed and payment given for them, and a long queue of prospectors waiting patiently to get their precious finds examined.

Every morning, Sam reminded us both to make sure our goggles fitted properly before we began working with the sheets. This particular day there was a dust cloud brewing in the distance.

"Any ideas what that is, Yorkie?" Sam asked pointing over to the dust cloud. I shrugged in reply and carried on climbing up to the roof. Sam followed me and powered-up the metal-grinder. Suddenly he screamed out. I rushed over to him and saw his goggles had slipped; hands pressed over his eyes. I grabbed his arm and hand to steady him.

"I'm blind – a spaaaarrghhk," he wheezed before screaming again. A couple of blokes heard his screams and helped us get down off the roof. I could feel my chest thumping away. *Shit, shit, shit, shit* was all I could think until my instincts took over.

"Where's the nearest doctor?" I shouted at the blokes.

"In a hamlet about five miles (eight kilometres) down the road," they returned, pointing the way. Sam was still screaming. We tried to wash his eye with some bottled water but that made the pain worse, to the point where he nearly passed out.

"Sam, listen to me, we'll get our gear from the hotel and get you to the nearest doctor, then we're going straight to the hospital in Perth, all right, me old china?" Sam's screaming turned into moaning; his hands still firmly clasped over his eyes. I managed to get him into the ute, then collected our gear from the hotel, and drove us out in the direction of the doctor's hamlet. This was in the same direction as the goldfields, and we passed the cloud of dust that perhaps had distracted Sam from checking his goggles. It was a dozen men on horseback carrying picks and shovels – I knew where they were headed for sure.

The five-mile drive to the hamlet took about half an hour over dusty, bumpy tracks. I kept patting Sam's arm.

"Hang in there, Cockney!" The doctor's house was easy to spot among the wooden shacks with its helpful sign 'Doctor here' over the door. I pulled-up outside, jumped out of the ute, ran to the door and barged through it without knocking. *Oh hell, if this was the doctor's there was no hope for anyone in this hamlet.* The stench of grog filled the air; the 'waiting' room was run down and dirty, and the 'doctor' appearing from the back room was no cleaner himself. I could see he was drunk, his filthy trousers and torn shirt barely covering his fat belly and judging by the smell of him he didn't like washing too often. But Sam was in a bad way, and I was desperate to get him help as fast as possible. The only choice we had at that moment was this deadbeat 'doc'.

He sat, or more like fell, onto a chair behind his desk that was itself only fit for a bonfire. He slurred when he spoke.

"Whassup, mate?"

I recounted the accident, and we went outside to fetch Sam from the ute and lay him down on the rickety table in the back room. The dishevelled doc took down some dirty-looking instruments from a cabinet – where I could see he stored empty, crumpled cans of grog - and prodded a long needle into Sam's eye. Sam screamed out in agony, almost falling onto the floor, but I just managed to catch hold and push him back onto the table. Sam screamed at me.

"Yorkie, keep him away from me!"

With that, something inside me snapped. I turned to the 'doctor' and shouted, "Keep doing that and he'll go blind you fat fuck!" I shoved the quack aside; he was so drunk he fell over onto the floor in a stupor. This drunken deadbeat should have been struck off the medical register years ago. I was fuming. I got Sam back to the ute and we set off on our six-hour road trip to Perth hospital.

I was sure we had enough gas in the tank to get us back to Perth without stopping, but I stopped a few times anyway to give Sam a drink of water and give him a rest from the bumping of the tracks. My Cockney mate was made of strong stuff, but it was clear he was struggling to keep the pain under control. He laid back in the ute with his hands over his eyes and every now and then he let out a groan.

"Hang-in there, lad," I kept saying as much to myself as to Sam. The drive seemed to last a lifetime but eventually we pulled-up outside the hospital. I ran in to fetch a doctor or nurse and told them everything that happened, including our trip to the drunkard in the outback. They soon got Sam inside, examined his eye and began some sort of treatment, I didn't really know what it was, but I could see it was giving Sam some welcome relief from the pain. After a few hours he was picking-up and looking a bit more like his old self.

The medical staff said a fragment of hot metal from the grinder had burnt a corner of Sam's eye causing an injury that would leave a scar. I couldn't help but wonder if the hamlet quack had caused the damage. The hospital doctor wanted to monitor Sam overnight and urged him to stay, but he wasn't having it.

"I'm leaving with you, Yorkie," he said, almost grinning - a good sign he was feeling better.

"You're very lucky you didn't lose your sight, Sam," a doctor told him. Turning to me he added, "if he has any more pain bring him straight back here."

After several hours we walked out of the hospital together into the late evening air. Sam said he wanted to spend the night at Graylands with me, Margaret and Dale and go home to his family in the morning. Margaret was still awake when we reached hut 129D, and at first was worried to see us because we weren't due back for at least another three days. Then she was shocked by the sight of Sam's face with one of his eyes patched-up. I gave her a hug and told her everything that happened that day. By this time, Sam was ready for a cup of tea and a sandwich. Margaret said she was going to bed and took Dale with her, leaving Sam and me chatting through the night. I think Sam wanted to stay with us in case the pain got worse. I could drive him to the hospital whereas if he went home Maureen would have to drive him and take their two daughters along with them. I think also, he was protecting his family from seeing him in such a bad way.

When dawn broke, I drove us over to Sam's house. Naturally, Maureen was shocked to see and hear what had happened and told us that, when we got back to Perth, we should have first called at their house before going to the hospital. Sam and I said nothing. I kept the ute for a few days until Sam got back on his feet again. Driving back to my family I wondered how many more times Sam could be lucky – he had had two accidents in the last few months that could have ended with him dead or crippled for life. Thinking that 'things' often came in threes, I wondered if, when the next time Sam said he had a job for us, I would say 'yes' because although I liked working with this Cockney Brit, there was no way I wanted a repeat of our recent experiences!

CHAPTER 15

Time for a change of career

I heard through the roofers' grapevine that some other contractors completed the job up towards the goldfield that Sam and I didn't finish. I didn't mind because we got paid for the work we did. During his recovery, an eye specialist told Sam that everything was healing well, and that he was very, very lucky that he still had sight in his damaged eye. It was obvious he wouldn't be working for at least a few more weeks. Margaret wasn't happy about me taking another job in the outback and I didn't want to upset her and our unborn baby, so I went back to NuRoof to do a few jobs around Perth. One of the other big perks of working locally - apart from getting to come home at the end of a day's shift - was once again having the use of a ute at the weekends. NuRoof didn't mind as long as the ute's tank was full on a Monday morning. On Margaret's free weekends we explored different beaches further away from Perth, giving Dale a chance to practise surfing.

Back on Graylands, more of our friends were heading to the eastern side of Australia to try their luck over there. Even when they bought their own caravans, they couldn't take everything they had accumulated while living on the camp with them, and often advertised the stuff they didn't want on the noticeboards dotted around the site. Margaret and I used to read them regularly in case there was something we could use.

There were also adverts for houses-for-sale or to rent, and even adverts for jobs. Around this time there was a lot of building going on in the centre of Perth, and adverts appeared on the noticeboards for bricklayers, labourers, and labourers used to working at heights. The wages were good, and workers were picked up from the camp and taken into Perth each morning and dropped-off again at the end of the day. I thought about it but at that moment was happy enough with the local roofing jobs. Most of the time they were easy and, when my workmate and I knew we could get everything done well within in a day, we took a sneaky siesta during the hottest part of the day, finishing the job as the sun descended from its highest point. We rigged-up a canopy at the back of the ute using old sacking and had a kip under there in the cool of the shade. Other days we needed to work on through the midday heat to get the job finished, and reckoned that we earnt every cent we got, siesta or no.

Working like this was fine but it wasn't earning the money we needed to save to pay for our fares back home - if returning home is what we wanted to do. Jobs were easy-come, easy-go and you could finish one job by mid-morning and get signed-up with another firm by the end of the day. It felt good to have a choice of work but not much of it paid well.

I was getting a bit fed-up going backwards and forwards to work in the hot sun, and also with living in the Nissen hut, whereas Margaret and Dale were still okay living on the camp and often seemed to be enjoying themselves. Dale had plenty of friends and was always going off on his own adventures around the camp. We knew he was safe because there were loads of families across the camp looking out for the kids. Dale made sure he got back to collect his knife, fork and spoon in time for the evening meal, as he knew he wouldn't get much off our plates, especially now Margaret was eating for two. I wasn't as happy being here as they were, and got more homesick when I saw more of our friends leaving the camp.

I saw the advert again for the Perth building jobs and all I needed to do was leave a message at the camp office with all the usual details, plus a description of my labouring experience. I heard that a few other Poms on site left their details, but I didn't, I just thought about it some more. Maybe because it meant changing from roofing work and I knew I was doing that well, even though I was a bit tired of it, plus there was plenty of work with NuRoof at that time.

I don't know how he got to know about me, but a few days after seeing the advert for the second time, there was a knock on the door of our hut. A Welsh bloke – we'd not seen him before – asked me if I had heard about the work in Perth and told me he was a bricklayer looking for a Pom labourer to heft bricks for him. I can understand nowadays how labelling people according to where they came from sounds prejudiced, but it wasn't at the time. Truth is, I've always been hopeless with names and even nowadays call my kids by each other's names before I get the right one. Naming people according to their country or county, even, was a recognition and nod to our different and proud heritages. What was important was to understand the words we spoke to each other especially with our workmates, and to get their attention quickly, which for me meant giving them a label that I could easily remember. It was easier and safer to be on a job with a workmate when you could understand what they said to you, and they understood what you said to them.

Anyway, this Welsh bloke became 'Taffy' (number two) to me and (as usual) I became 'Yorkie' to him. Taffy was married with kids, and they'd been on the camp for about nine months. He had had a few building jobs but, like most of us, found the money wasn't good. He had a plan to save for a few years, get enough to buy a piece of land and then build a bungalow on it. I liked him.

"Ok, Taffy, I'm in!" *Well, like-it-or-not,* I thought, *my career is about to change, again*!

Taffy told me to leave my details at the camp office. A few days later I got a note from the building company telling me to be on site with Taffy in a couple of days. That weekend Margaret, Dale and me, we all met Taffy's wife and two sons – they were both a bit older than Dale, but they seemed to all get on okay. Monday came, Taffy picked me up and drove us in his ute to the worksite in the centre of Perth. I couldn't believe my eyes! It was amazing, what with scores of workers everywhere, cranes lifting materials from one place to another, a good supply of water, proper toilet cabins and even official breaktimes!

Taffy and I were given a couple of hours to get used to the site, check out what-was-what and then our real work began. My job was to fetch mortar, breeze blocks and other building materials from the crane buckets over to Taffy, where he was laying the blocks as fast as I could get them wheel-barrowed over to him. The graft was hard but one of the bonuses of working in the city was being in the shade of the tall buildings, which made it a lot cooler for us than the exposed conditions in the outback. We were classed as 'casual workers' and were paid cash-in-hand at the end of the week. I was knackered by then and slept a lot but it was good money and the dollars started to pile-up.

I found out that the building Taffy and I were working on was destined to become a block of luxury apartments. The top floor would have 360° views across the city and beyond and would become the suite to accommodate visiting ambassadors and dignitaries. Taffy and me, we worked well together, and I soon picked up the pace to keep Taffy and a couple of other brickies supplied with breeze blocks, mortar and any other materials they needed. The floors of every block on site were concrete and around and over that, scaffolding was erected bit-by-bit to keep ahead of the growing buildings. We worked on timber board platforms laid across the scaffolding, and sometimes climbed into the bucket attached by a chain to the crane to hitch a ride up to the level where we were working. I can't remember how many floors the finished building would have, but I just remember it was a lot.

Taffy and me, we were getting on well outside of work too. On our weekends off, Taffy and family used to come to our hut and we'd share a few grogs. One time we were sitting outside chatting when suddenly, Taffy screamed, jumped to his feet and dropped his shorts. His wife – I forgot her name - asked him what was wrong.

"A spider – up my leg," he shouted, hopping around shaking each leg free of his shorts. The rest of us couldn't help but laugh. Then Taffy's wife took over, checking his shorts and shaking them out. With that, a spider dropped out and scuttled away, though not very far before I stamped on it, squashing it underneath my flip-flop.

Naturally, Taffy thought he had been bitten but his wife checked him over and found no evidence of a bite, she clouted him round the ear.

"Get your shorts on and make yourself decent you dozy beggar, or else we won't be invited here again!"

The following morning Taffy was waiting outside in his ute as usual.

"Do you think I got bitten, Yorkie?"

"If you did, Taff, you wouldn't be talking to me now!" He laughed and started whistling the Welsh national anthem. Taffy was easy to spot on the building site because he always wore his over-sized hat, which, as well as tassels hanging down from it, had a big felt daffodil sewn on to one side. He told me his wife had made the daffodil and sewn it on, and he wore the hat everywhere he worked over there. He said he would wear it until it fell to pieces, which was easy to believe.

One morning, I was waiting for Taffy to appear in his ute but there wasn't the usual knock on the door. I wondered where he had got to, so I went round to his hut and found there was no ute parked-up and the hut looked empty. I didn't know what had happened, but it looked like the whole family had gone, cleared out. I came across the duty manager and asked him about Taffy and family. He told me they had given notice to leave at the weekend, that they were going over to the eastern side of Australia to try their luck there. He didn't know they'd done a moonlight flit but wasn't angry which meant they must have been all squared-up with the rent. I was gutted. I thought we got on well and I couldn't understand why he hadn't said anything to me.

Margaret said, "Maybe he felt bad about letting you down and didn't want any emotional goodbyes."

This made me feel a bit better and then I remembered seeing their knives, forks and spoons set out in place on the table ready and waiting to get stuck into a meal. Somehow, it felt like a message to me, a shared joke about the importance of our own cutlery sets, given to us on arrival at the camp. This cheered me up and I chuckled to myself, *Good luck Taff and family*! I wished them well and hoped I would spot Taffy's hat again, somewhere, someday.

The next morning, I was up early and back on the train to Perth. At the city centre construction site, the foreman called me over and told me Taffy had been paid and was on his travels, and from now on I would be labouring for a gang of German bricklayers. They were laying the bricks on the outside of the building to cover the breeze blocks, and they worked non-stop because they were on a bonus. I managed to keep up with their pace of work but felt like a lost soul among them. I like to chat, it's the banter with my workmates that made a lot of these jobs bearable. I knew I was getting miserable and felt like walking off the site but kept thinking about the pay packet at the end of the week, and the money building up in our savings account. This kept me going.

At the end of the second day's shift, I was about to pack-up when I could smell bitumen heating-up, and to my surprise heard Richard's voice and a couple of other workers from NuRoof. I went over to say 'Hello,' and they told me the firm had been given the job of felting the roof of one of the tall

74

tower blocks. They also said that they were short-staffed again and were having trouble finding workers to sign-up for jobs in the outback. I felt my spirits rising at the thought of being back among some familiar faces and was excited to tell all of this to Margaret. When I did, I could see she wasn't happy, but I stressed how with Taffy disappearing I felt lost on the building site.

The next day I told the foreman I'd be finished by the end of the week and asked him to get my wages ready. He said that was a shame, he was sorry to see me go because he'd had good reports about me from the German brickies. He even said he'd increase my wages by a few dollars an hour. I was tempted to stay but not for long – I wanted to be back on familiar territory with the lads at the roofing firm. After leaving my new career as a brickie's labourer behind, I've often wondered since if the tower blocks I worked on are still the tallest in Perth, or if they've been overtaken by others; they probably have by now.

CHAPTER 16

Back to roofing and a Great Escape

The next week there I was again, back working at the local roofing firm. Back to working with hot bitumen; it didn't seem to matter how careful you were when handling it – a skill in itself – you always ended up with a few burns and blisters on the hands and legs. I had the use of a ute again and along with it the job of picking-up some of the workers on the way to NuRoof's yard. My work-buddy was Bruno and it was good to see him again. Most of our jobs were local until one day we were given a job further afield towards Coolgardie to refelt the roof of a low-risk prison for reforming or rehabilitating ex-offenders. The job was expected to take a couple of weeks.

Our hotel accommodation in Coolgardie (the 'Denver City Hotel' still stands in 2023)

Both of us had worked in or near Coolgardie before and were used to the rough tracks and dusty driving conditions when we left the solid roads behind. We got booked into a hotel in the town, which was a couple of miles from the prison, and decided we should go take a look at the worksite. The prison's driveway leading to its main security gates was about half a mile long down a dusty track lined both sides with lifeless and leafless white trees. Hanging from one of the highest branches was the figure of a dummy swaying backwards and forwards with a noose around its neck and a large, printed notice fixed to the tree trunk.

"Hey, Bruno look at that!" I said, pointing at the notice, "see that sign, it says, 'All are welcome here!' Some bloody welcome that is!" I felt a bit spooked, and Bruno looked a bit worried too. I swear the dummy's dead eyes followed us as we made our way down the drive to the prison.

We were directed to stop at the gates by two guards, and Bruno showed them the papers he'd been given by NuRoof. We were then told to get out of the ute while they carried out a thorough search – looking under the seats, the bonnet, the wheel rims and all over for any nooks and crannies where something might be hidden. When they finished searching the ute they asked us to empty our pockets. I found the whole thing a scary experience – wasn't it supposed to be a low-risk, reforming prison? I was getting worried about the conditions we'd be working in once inside those gates. Satisfied we weren't trying to smuggle anything into the prison, the guards opened the gates waving us through.

We were met by a couple of prison officers who showed us to our worksite up on the roof, and on the way there we passed a lot of prisoners lolling around, every other one seemed to be an Aborigine. I began to feel a bit more relaxed when I saw there were ladders and a lift for us to use. The Australian prison officers told us where the toilet blocks where, that we could use the canteen free-of-charge, and if we needed anything to ask them. They went out of their way to help us and we were grateful for that. I wondered if they ever felt like prisoners themselves: at the start of their shift, they were locked inside the prison and couldn't leave until the end of the shift when they were released. It's not a job I could do. Working outside I could come and go whenever I wanted, I was free and couldn't bear the thought of being locked in every day. The time it took us to refelt the prison roof was a long enough stretch in the clink for me!

After Bruno and I had fetched our work gear one of the officers asked if we wanted to take a look around. There seemed to be quite a lot of friendly banter between the prisoners and the guards, but the prisoners were told to keep away from any workers coming in from the outside. The prison compound covered quite a big area and consisted of a canteen, toilet and shower blocks and a workshop. The atmosphere was quite relaxed.

I asked one of the officers, "Does anyone ever go missing?"

He turned to me laughing. "Look over that high fence, mate, what do you see? What is there to escape to? Nothing!" It's true, the land we'd driven through to get here was barren and lacking in cover to hide escapees. He went on to tell us that often when the prisoners were getting close to their release date, they would start a fight to get more time inside because that's where they felt safe. He also said that most inmates were heavy grog-drinkers who had caused trouble when drunk.

I noticed the inmates seemed quite happy in the workshop, some whistling while they worked. There were shelves displaying their craftsmanship: boomerangs, wooden figures, soft toys and Aboriginal-looking paintings. The officer said these craftworks were sold on the outside to raise money for people worse off than the inmates, I wondered who they might be! Seeing those soft toys gave me an idea and a plan began to hatch.

Back at the hotel Bruno asked me if I wanted to go for a bevvie or two, which took me by surprise coming from the man who said grog was bad for you. Of course, I didn't remind him of his previous comments, I just enjoyed what was on offer. On our walk from the hotel to the bar we passed a small shop that sold all sorts of things from chocolate bars to jewellery. It was a funny set-up, a large wooden frame – obviously living quarters - built over an enclosed yard, to this day I don't know how it held together, which is maybe why I noticed it in the first place. We got talking about the prison job and worked out that it wouldn't take as long as we first thought, which made me decide to put my plan into action as soon as possible.

On our second day arriving at the prison gates, the guards were more relaxed with their search and were even friendly. They continued to be this way every following day. One day after we'd had a break for a bit of lunch,

Bruno decided to have a siesta in the shaded area of the roof, and I decided to go off for a wander around the prison. An officer gave me the okay and off I went, calling first at the workshop, where I found an inmate happily whistling as he went about his work.

Since first spotting the soft toys sitting on the workshop shelf, I had wanted one for our soon-to-appear baby daughter (fingers crossed!) I asked the inmate if I could buy one and he said no, not for money because they weren't allowed any, but a few bars of chocolate would be nice. He went on to tell me there was a travelling shop that visited them about once a month, where they could exchange any chits they had received for good behaviour for shop produce such as bars of chocolate. This told me that something as humble as a chocolate bar meant a lot to these inmates. The chap could see I was hatching a plan to get one of the soft toys because he told me which day one of the easy-going prison officers was on duty. Now I knew what I needed to do to get my daughter one of these little beauts.

On the drive back to our digs I told Bruno about my plan; being a man of very high principles, he said,

"What I do not see, I do not know!" He meant I was on my own, but at least he didn't try and persuade me not to go ahead. I left the hotel and walked over to the strange-looking shop, and there I bought a few bars of chocolate. I put them in a small cool bag and hid them in the passenger seat-well of the ute, feeling confident the guards wouldn't search in there again. That night I slept badly thinking *what if they do search under the seat? I could end-up in prison myself making soft toys!*

On the following day's long drive down to the prison gates the dummy was swaying about from its noose and I swear it was pointing in my direction.

"Did you see that, Bruno? Did you see the dummy swaying?" I asked.

"Yes," he said, "but why it sways when there is no wind?" giving me a knowing look. We said no more about it. The officer on duty smiled and chatted as he checked the back of the ute, he opened the gates with a friendly,

"It's going to be a real scorcher for you on the roof today, lads." Phew! First hurdle passed!

After lunch Bruno took a siesta and I went a-wandering again, first outside to the ute to get some 'gear' that I then hid under my hat. Next call was the workshop where once again I saw the whistling craftsman who smiled when he saw me. We chatted a bit to make sure I hadn't been followed or was being watched – this was the days before cctv.

After a while I said, "Well, I'd better get back to work, good day to you!" and swept my hat off my head bringing it down low so he could see the chocolate bars inside. Quick-as-a-flash he grabbed them and tucked them away before I could see where they had gone.

"Cheers, bunji! Meet you in the canteen," he said, grinning.

I was feeling nervous and was sure I had a guilty look on my face, but was buzzing from the excitement of this daring little adventure as I made my way to the canteen. It was a large room with a piano in one corner, several inmates and officers were scattered about in small groups, chatting, and a few inmates behind the counter were making cups of tea. The Aborigine craftsman from the workshop walked over to the piano and began playing 'Waltzing Matilda.' The piano needed retuning but was good enough for me to recognise the song. I walked over and joined in on the high notes using what was left of the keys. Bruno appeared in the doorway and came over to join us at the piano.

"I do not know you play music," he said.

"I play by ear," I replied tugging at my right ear. Bruno looked a bit puzzled, "I can't read music, but I can pick up a tune ok".

"Ah! Good!" he said, "Now we get back to work!" Bruno began walking out of the canteen, the pianist and I following close behind.

"I'll see you in a few minutes," I said to Bruno. He replied with a nod getting my drift. On our way back to the workshop, the pianist-craftsman told me he was a long-term inmate and life-long alcoholic. He was a very skilled man who didn't get a chance in life to make something of himself, something more than being a long-term inmate. But I have to say he seemed happy enough with his lot.

When we reached the workshop, he said, "Take your pick, bunji."

"Now, which one will my daughter like?" I asked and chose a small teddy bear with a yellow ribbon around his neck, popping him under my hat. I shook the craftsman's hand and away I went to rejoin Bruno on the roof. The little bear stayed under my hat for the rest of the afternoon.

I was glad when we finished-up for the day and were driving away from the prison gates, back down the long driveway having been waved on through by the prison guards. Even the dummy looked less evil and had stopped swaying about on its noose. By the time we got back to the hotel I was shattered but very pleased with myself. My plan had worked and I had got my baby girl her first present, I was feeling like a good dad!

When we arrived at the prison gates the following day we weren't stopped and checked at all, just waved through. This time after lunch Bruno came for a stroll around the grounds with me. We walked around the perimeter fence watching a few kangaroos hopping about in the distance, then headed back to the canteen drawn there by the music played on the out-of-tune piano. The same piano-craftsman was playing, and I rejoined him on the high notes. He smiled and said he played almost every day. His music made me homesick for Old Blighty, and I wondered if it had the same effect on him for his home.

"Come with me, bunji," he said getting up from the piano and leaving the canteen. I followed him to the workshop where he popped in and then back out holding another small teddy bear, this one had a pink ribbon around its neck.

"Two chocolate bars – two toys." I thanked him and popped the bear under my hat. On our drive back to the hotel Bruno asked me if I'd got what I wanted from the workshop.

"How you know Margaret will have baby girl?"

I lifted my hat, removed the little bear with the pink ribbon and waved it at him.

"Look, it's pink for a girl! I didn't tell the craftsman I wanted pink for a baby daughter, he chose it himself because he *knows* the baby will be a girl!" I'm not sure I believed what I was saying but it seemed to convince Bruno.

"Ok," he nodded, "she will be little girl."

The next day was our final day on the job and the last time I saw the piano-craftsman. I wonder if he was ever released. We finished the job a few hours after lunch and got the manager to sign it off, then we loaded our gear. I took one last look around feeling sad about leaving because the officers and inmates had treated us really well.

We passed through the prison gates for the final time but not before everything was thoroughly searched one last time, which made me sweat a bit – what would have happened if they'd searched us like this yesterday and found the bear? Driving back down the prison driveway I said to Bruno,

"That dummy's been turned around and look, he's smiling!" Bruno peered through the rear-view mirror and just shook his head.

We stayed at the hotel that night to make an early start back home the next morning. After we had something to eat we walked over to the bar to share a few grogs. Bruno opened up a bit and told me about his life growing-up in Poland. He had many brothers and sisters, his father was a lumberjack, his mother a housewife and they all lived together in a log cabin at the edge of the forest where their father worked. Bruno and his brothers and sisters used to play in the forest building dens, swimming in the local lakes and caring for the chickens they raised for eggs and meat. I could see and hear how much he missed his homeland and wondered if that's why he was against the grog, or used to be, because it made him think about the past and pine for home.

I asked him how he came to be in Western Australia, but he clammed-up and turned away from me. I changed the subject quickly. "Ah well, better be getting back to the hotel – early to bed means early start tomorrow?" Bruno nodded and we turned in for the night. *Bruno, old chap*, I thought to myself, *whatever drove you from your homeland to come here will keep you from ever going back to live there again*. I felt sad for him and selfishly, happy for me, because I knew the only thing preventing me and my family from returning to Britain (if that's we eventually wanted to do), was money for the ticket fares, and that was something Margaret and I were both working on.

CHAPTER 17

Winter becomes spring (September to November) and brings the prospect of a new home, a visit to the zoo and a wonderful meal

The following morning, we were away with an early start back to Graylands. I walked through the door of our hut to find Margaret and Dale eating their lunch.

"Hope you saved some for me!'" I said, giving Margaret a hug and ruffling the top of Dale's head. It was good to be back with my family again. I told them about the prison adventure with the soft toys.

"You daft beggar," said Margaret, "they wouldn't have locked you up for buying a couple of teddy bears!" Dale laughed, maybe she was right, but she hadn't been there in the prison to know what was acceptable and what wasn't. Anyway, I wasn't taking any chances.

There had been some new and exciting activity since I left; there were construction workers on site building some new accommodation blocks. We heard it was possible to get a transfer from the huts to one of the new flats if you had a valid reason. We thought what better reason could there be than being pregnant, so we filled out an application form and kept our fingers crossed.

New families were arriving at Graylands, and others were leaving to either go back to their homelands or follow the trail of immigrants from the western to the eastern states to look for better opportunities, like Taffy and family did. Margaret said she heard a new family from England had recently arrived and we should go and make them feel welcome. They arrived on site a few hours after landing in Australia and told us they were glad to have their feet on solid ground again. We gave them a tour of the camp showing them the toilet and shower blocks and the play area for kids of all ages – they had two sons a bit older than Dale.

Eventually, we reached the canteen and found a large notice on the door 'NO KNIFE, FORK AND SPOON – NO MEAL!!' We knew about this rule but hadn't noticed this sign before. Perhaps it had been put up for all the new arrivals. Perhaps many of those who left the camp, kept their cutlery as mementoes and the camp manager had to keep forking out(!) to buy new sets! This new family hadn't been issued with theirs yet, so we took them along to the camp office and explained what they needed to do to get their very own, precious cutlery set.

I can't remember their names now, but I do remember the new family were from Kent. The husband was a builder or was used to working on building sites, and I told him he shouldn't have any trouble finding work over here. I said I'd been working with a local roofing-firm for about a year now and could try and get him fixed-up with something to tide him over until work more to his liking came along.

"Thanks," he said, "but the only thing is, I'm no good working at heights. I get vertigo." Well, there might be something he could do, so I would ask anyway. We took them along to meet some of the other Poms on site and hoped they would soon be feeling less lost and alone. We'd all been through that stage and knew it was a big relief to find others who had felt the same and had come out the other side.

I continued to work at NuRoof but without the ute for a while, just doing some general work around the yard. One day, who did I see in the office but Sam. I was pleased to think he felt ready to get back to work and went over to catch-up with him.

"Eh up Cockney, how's it going?" I asked, shaking his hand.

"Hello there, Yorkie lad," he replied, smiling, "how are you doing?" His injured eye still looked puffy and sore to me, but he said he'd been discharged from the hospital's care. We arranged for Sam and family to come over to Graylands at the weekend, which happened to be one of Margaret's free ones. We would all spend some time at Cottesloe Beach, each family bringing along a hamper packed with cool drinks.

When I returned home that night, I told Margaret and she said we should invite the new arrivals too, so I popped round to their hut and told them the plan. That weekend saw six adults and five kids spend a smashing day on the beach. Sam and family got on well with the new arrivals from Kent and even the kids played together without falling out. *This is good, I thought* and maybe for a whole day I forgot about feeling homesick.

On Margaret's next weekend off, Sam came over in his family car, picked the three of us up and drove back to his house to collect Maureen and the girls, and away we all went to Perth Zoo. By 1968 the zoo had been around for seventy years and was a popular destination for tourists and locals alike. The gardens were amazing and looked lush with many tall trees that had green leaves – a sight hardly seen since we left Blighty – providing some welcome shaded areas to sit and enjoy a picnic. A park notice explained that water was pumped from the Swan River to keep everything looking healthy. I think it was also used to fill the children's paddling pool that Dale and Sam's two girls were splashing about in. The river water must have been cleaned too, because it looked a lot better in the paddling pool than when Dale and I went for a swim in the river a few months back.

As well as the paddling pool, the kids loved looking at the animals. I think that was the first time Dale saw orangutans and he kept asking me why they were orange. We also saw Tricia the elephant from Vietnam who was in a compound on her own. I wondered if she felt homesick because she didn't look happy, but she must have got used to the zoo eventually because she only recently died (July 2022).

I remember there were some bear caves, tennis grounds and even some mineral baths, plus mobile ice-cream trucks where we all treated ourselves to some lovely, cool, Italian ice-cream. Margaret got a double portion to cool her down because she was feeling the heat more and more and it made her feel very tired. Soon our daughter (fingers crossed!) would be born and we would all come back here as a family of four. Before we knew it, it was time to leave, and I realised that was another day when I hadn't felt at all homesick.

Sam dropped us off at Graylands. When Margaret and Dale were back in the hut, he said it was about time he got back to work, and asked me if I would like to join him in the outback if a job turned up. I knew Margaret wasn't keen and I didn't want to leave her and Dale alone for so long, but at the same time I didn't want to let Sam down so I said.

"At the moment I can't say yes or no, what with Margaret and the baby."

"Don't worry, Yorkie, let's see how things go." With that we shook hands and away he went. Margaret's pregnancy wasn't the only reason I was keen to stay close, Dale was causing her a lot of stress too because he kept wandering off and she worried about him. She explained to him that he needed to tell her where he was going but he didn't take any notice. When I spoke to him about how he would soon have a baby sister (fingers crossed), and that he would need to help his mum look after her, he said, "Ok!" and went running out of the hut to find his mates.

Dale must have explored every nook and cranny of Graylands. Although we knew it was safe on site and that he had lots of good friends, we worried about him being outside and vulnerable to attack by flying ants, biting spiders, scorpions and snakes. Luckily though, he usually managed to return home unharmed, except for the times when he was struck by a catapulted bullet, and his head got pecked by a bird!

I thought if I was around more, Margaret wouldn't be alone so much and might not get so worried about Dale. Her boss at the hospital was very good to her, always making sure she only did light duties on her shift, so at least there were no worries there. I knew it was important to try and keep her calm and free from worries as much as possible, for her health and the baby's. Poor Margaret had had a terrible time giving birth to Dale, and we didn't want that to happen again.

One day, Margaret came home from work with an invitation from Carol and Neville to go out for a meal to celebrate Carol's birthday. Our friends from Liverpool offered to look after Dale for the night, so we were all set to go and were ready when Neville came to pick us up. He and Carol chose a restaurant in King's Park on the outskirts of Perth. The park covered the top of a mound with views across the Swan River and causeway, and the park itself was full of well-kept trees, bushes and lovely coloured flowers, none of which we had seen before. The area looked very posh to us; the restaurant was in the park and had its own well-kept grounds.

We were seated at a table for four with brilliant views over the city, across the river and out to the causeway. There were lots of insects buzzing about, especially mosquitoes but they were drawn away from the diners to the lamps burning some sort of fragrant oil. By the time we got served, the night had drawn in and the dark blue sky was lit with the glitter of millions of stars. As if in response, the lights in the city came on and the lights below the park outlined the causeway and were reflected in the Swan River. It was a truly magical night – I can picture it now.

The evening got even better when we ate crayfish for the first (and only) time. It was the most delicious food Margaret and I had ever tasted in our lives. We went the whole hog that night with desserts, iced coffee and a few grogs for me and Neville to finish. All four of us had a great night and chatted away. Carol was interested in Britain, especially Hull because her parents came over to Australia from Hull before she was born.

We finished the evening with a nightcap at their house. After Neville drove us home, we collected Dale and told him all about our time at the restaurant and the twinkling stars and lights. It must have been the magic of the moment because sitting there in the posh restaurant was one of the few occasions when I wondered if I really wanted to go back to England. For all its charms and my deep love for my homeland, I had never experienced anything as special as that evening we spent with our friends in King's Park.

CHAPTER 18

Spring brings rain and a wheely bad experience

By now it was the rainy season and with it came some very heavy downpours, although they only lasted about an hour each time. What a relief they were from the rising heat that increased as spring progressed. The rain soaked the ground but it quickly dried-up again. Some of the water must have seeped further down into the earth to water the vegetation, because the plants began to spring into life. Back in Old Blighty it was autumn and the trees were losing their leaves, and the hedgerows dying back. Hedgerows? They were a rare sight over here. I was probably thinking of hedgerows from something in one of Elsie's regular letters and enclosed newspaper clippings. They were good to read but sometimes made me feel homesick, especially when I thought of Elsie and Bill's place at Hutton Cranswick, surrounded by green fields, and trees full of birds around the village pond.

I was still without the ute and back to travelling every day on the steam train to NuRoof, where I saw Sam a few times and we always waved to each other. I was sure he was working in the outback again because he had another bloke with him who I didn't recognise at all, which meant he wasn't working locally, or I would have seen him around. People coming-and-going all the time was the way of things over there. I was back with Richard and we worked together on local jobs.

One day I realised that I hadn't seen Bruno in a while and asked Richard where he was and what he was up to. I was told he was sick and had been in the hospital from a spider-bite that happened on a job and needed some time to recover. Richard's English wasn't as good as Bruno's so I never got the full story, but I grasped the incident had unnerved Bruno. Of course, I didn't mention any of this to Margaret because I didn't want her to worry about what might happen to me on the job. Sam's incidents were scary enough for all of us, she didn't need to hear about any more work-related accidents.

After about a week or so of local work, I was given the ute again because Richard and I were assigned a felting job on the Perth side of Kalgoorlie. It meant staying away from home, but Kalgoorlie wasn't that far – less than

400 miles (640 kilometres) from Perth - and it was only a week's work, maybe less.

The felt we were given to use was new to the market. Richard and I were called into the office and instructed how to handle the new material. We were told to be very vigilant because there was an Aborigine settlement close to the worksite, and there were a lot of thefts and trouble due to drunkenness. I couldn't blame the poor buggers from what I'd seen of where they lived, but we had a job to do and needed to be careful, nonetheless.

I picked Richard up the following morning and off we set on another dusty drive. First, we went to check out the worksite before booking into our hotel. The building was a storage warehouse - not very high but my, what a length. We knew straightaway that we'd need more bitumen and felt than we'd brought with us to complete the job. Our ladders reached to the top of the building right up to the roof, and from there we could see the Aborigine settlement. I was distracted from the view by the sounds of shouting down below.

"Look Richard! They're stealing our materials." And sure enough, a group of Aborigine men were grabbing stuff from the back of the ute. Luckily, there were some other workers on site who shouted and ran over to the ute to chase them away. If they hadn't, we would have lost everything by the time we got down from the roof.

The hotel was a class one by virtue of its telephone, and Richard made use of it to order more materials from NuRoof. That evening, we had a couple of grogs and I told the hotel manager (who was also the barman) what had happened earlier. He said we could store all of our tools and materials at the back of the hotel, but there was no space for the ute. Suddenly, there was a lot of shouting and swearing coming from a small room at the back of the bar.

"I know what's going on in there," I said to Richard, "let's take a look!" We opened the door on a dozen or so gamblers shouting at their cockroaches to scuttle to the opposite end of the bar and win the race. We took one look at the size of the 'roaches and scuttled on out of there ourselves, they were bloody enormous!

On our first day on the job we removed all the old felting, which was sometimes the hardest part of the work. This one was made harder because we couldn't leave any tools on site else they'd all be gone by morning. By the end of the day, we'd stripped most of the felt, chucking it off the roof as we went along and leaving it on the ground. Below. On driving away from the worksite, I noticed a few Aborigine men hanging about and watching our every move, I pulled over and looked back.

"Look, Richard they're taking away the rotten felt!"

"Good, we not do it!" He replied, grinning. That's true, one less job for us!

The hotel was the best I remember staying in but very basic by today's standards. Back then having an indoor shower was a luxury. Richard phoned the roofing firm again to make sure we would get the drums of bitumen and felt within the next few days. The firm sent trucks packed with materials out on delivery to several sites within an area, and they confirmed ours would soon arrive. The next few days on the job were okay, the weather was humid (but bearable) and the work was straightforward once we had stripped-off and cleared all of the old felt.

In the distance we could see utes and trucks trundling along the dust tracks at the end of the Great Eastern highway over to the goldfields at Coolgardie. I often wondered if any of the hopeful gold diggers ever struck a find that was more than a few small nuggets. It must have been worth the effort for many of them, else why would they keep going there to try their luck?

We arrived back at the hotel at sundown in time to see a posse of chaps ride up to the hotel and tie their horses on a rail outside the hotel entrance. I recognised them as the cockroach gamblers we first heard, then saw in the bar on our first night and every night since. They got louder and louder as the night and the gambling wore on, eventually shouting and swearing and often coming to blows. Their presence made me want to get the job done as fast as possible and get back to Graylands. This was the Wild West of Australia, without the guns!

Richard and I were in the bar having our nightly one or two grogs when I heard barking coming from outside the back of the hotel. The hotel manager-barman said he kept a couple of large dogs – I forget the type, but they sounded big - for his personal safety. In the small hours of the following morning, I was woken by more barking that went on for ages with the hotel manager shouting at them to be quiet. I knew I should have got-up and looked outside, why would the dogs start barking at nothing? I was just too tired and comfortable. When I went outside the next morning the ute looked a bit low on the ground at its back end.

"Oh, Hell, must be a flat tyre," I said to Richard, then I looked a bit closer – a back wheel was missing! How on Earth that ute had been lifted high enough and for long enough to remove a wheel, I don't know. Of course, that's why the dogs had been barking and they probably disturbed the thieves, which is why they only managed to swipe one wheel. We were glad we had previously taken the hotel manager's advice and left a spare wheel along with our tools safely in his yard.

Richard and me, we agreed not to mention this incident to NuRoof, they probably wouldn't notice one missing spare wheel. After that incident we were very wary of everything we did, feeling we were being watched at all times, especially at the worksite where more Aborigine youths were gathering every day.

The following night we parked the ute out of sight, or so we thought. We were woken in the early hours by the sound of ferocious barking. This time we jumped up sharpish and ran outside – no-one to be seen but what did we find? This time the ute looked very low on the ground at the front and back, all four wheels had been removed and stolen! Of course, we knew who the culprits were. The hotel manager said he would phone the police to come over from Kalgoorlie. Richard had to make a phone call too, one we both dreaded – to the head office of NuRoof.

When Richard finished the phone conversation, he said Alec was on his way to us with replacement wheels. Alec also said that this would be the last job we would ever do for NuRoof. By this time, we had had enough and were ready to leave the job as it stood, until the hotel manager came up with an idea. He said we could use his old banger with a trailer attached, and he would tie one of his dogs in the back to make sure nothing got nicked. What a size that dog was, more like the size of a small horse than any dog I had ever seen, but he made us feel a bit more secure.

As the day rolled on into the early afternoon, we heard barking and looked down from the roof to see a group of Aborigine men approaching the car and trailer. They stopped a few feet away from the trailer when the dog was almost in a barking frenzy; they turned and scarpered, vanishing into the scrub. Richard and I turned to one another with the thumbs-up sign and carried on working. That evening the hotel manager said he would put two of his monster dogs in the bag of the wheel-less ute, "or she'll be left a shell by daybreak!" That did the trick, no more ute-raiding and stripping for parts that night.

By mid-afternoon the following day Alec arrived with replacement wheels. He jumped out of his ute ranting and raving from the off, waving his arms about. His face turned bright red and I thought he was going to have a fit. He was shouting as he came marching over to us.

"I told you what could happen out here, you idiots! You're damned to hell you stupid, flamin' galahs! You will both pay for the new tyres!" This got me riled.

"Look, we had nowhere to hide the ute!" I snapped back. "I'm hitching a ride back to Perth!" and started to walk away. Richard tried to calm things down, but his voice was so quiet he couldn't break through Alec's explosive damnations of us. Before I'd managed to walk many paces, Alec was calming down and Richard came running after me.

"Come back, Yorkie. Alec, he ok now. He know only you and me to finish the job, he need us, yes?" I knew that was true, we were the only two workers who could finish the job on time. I didn't want to let Richard down and reluctantly walked back with him to where Alec stood. He nodded to Richard and passed him an envelope or something like that, I wasn't sure what it was at the time. Later, at the hotel bar Richard insisted on paying for a couple of rounds of grogs, which made me think Alec passed him a few extra dollars in the envelope to get him to persuade me to finish the job. I'd had it with NuRoof, and made up my mind that they would soon be history.

CHAPTER 19

Spiders, dens, Big Bertha comes to live with us and an emotional roller-coaster ride

A few days later the job was finished and we were heading back to Perth. When I got back to Graylands I noticed some changes both on-site and at home: the new accommodation blocks were coming along at a good pace; Margaret's baby bump had grown, she looked tired and seemed a bit downbeat. I wondered if the shine of this way of life was wearing off for her. Dale was the same as ever and just carried on with his own adventures around the camp when he wasn't at school.

We didn't know it at the time, but the next few months were to be a period containing more ups-and-downs than the roller-coaster ride at Hull Fair. For example: Being back on camp and among our Pommie friends was good because it helped me feel settled, and we all enjoyed some great conversations about the different counties and cities we had lived in, but at the same time it made me feel homesick talking about the past. Then again, talk of home in Old Blighty gave us hope of setting foot back there someday.

One day, out of nowhere, our hut along with one or two others became infested by a plague of spiders that quickly spread to other huts across the camp. The insect sprayers appeared in force to try and keep them under control. They told us the change in temperature - as we headed from spring into summer - made the females seek out cooler spots where they could nest and have their young. I didn't realise how bad our infestation was until one day I heard Margaret screaming from inside the hut.

"Barrie, Barrie, come here, quick!" Followed by, "Thwack!" "Thwack!" "Squelch!" I rushed inside to find her waving a broom about hitting it over and over again on the floor. I looked down to see a swarm of tiny baby spiders scuttling away from the crushed body of their mother, who had accidentally become the victim of Margaret's foot as she innocently walked around the hut.

It was a horrible and amazing sight at the same time. These were called 'Wolf Spiders' and although would nip a person when they got too close, they weren't poisonous. They weren't very big either, but they scared a lot of the Poms judging by the number of times we heard screaming and saw people running away from their huts.

This spider episode upset everybody and brought down the general mood in our group of friends. Eventually, the huts were cleared and we began to relax a bit until Margaret had a scary experience at work. She opened one of the ward blinds and found herself face-to-face with a spider the size of her out-stretched hand. The poor lass froze with fear, staring at it terrified until a couple of staff appeared with a net to catch it.

Often on a Sunday when Margaret wasn't working, we would go for a walk around the camp, and usually Dale went off and did his own thing. One Sunday, I asked him where he vanished off to and what did he do.

"I'll show you, dad, come with me," and away we went on a tour of the site with a couple of his friends in-tow. That's when I discovered that Graylands was much bigger than I had ever realised, and that Dale had seen much more of it than we had. The land seemed to stretch on forever, and we came across more brick-built accommodation blocks well under construction. Would we be lucky enough to get one of those new apartments when our daughter was born? We were both now sure the baby was a girl and had even chosen a name for her. If the baby did turn out to be a boy we'd need to think again.

Back on our tour of the camp we had reached a clump of trees with a dodgy-looking swing attached to one of the branches. Dale was tugging at my arm.

"Look, dad" he said, proudly pointing to a makeshift den he and his mates had built.

"Good for you, son!" I said, pleased he was trying the outdoor life for himself, until I began thinking about all the insects that might join them in the den. He said the den was a shelter from the heat, and when I asked him what the nearby pile of sand was for, he said that eventually they would build their own huts. The sand looked very similar to the sand I'd just seen at the site where the new accommodation blocks were being built, but I didn't say anything, I was happy to see he was having a good time with his mates.

The last stop on our walk about camp was the noticeboard near the office; I liked looking at it to see what was on offer. On this occasion a 'very large' fridge was for sale from another family leaving Perth. Margaret and I went to take a look and bought it straight away. Having our own fridge meant we wouldn't need to be tied to the canteen for our meals, and we could enjoy cool drinks at any time. I asked a couple of Pommie mates if they would help me get the fridge from across camp and into our hut, and another bloke who was an electrician ('leccy') fixed it up for us. We told Dale he could have the honour of switching it on, like the Mayor of Hull switching on the town centre Christmas lights. He flicked the switch and the giant fridge hummed and thrummed into life, the thrumming increasing in volume until eventually it reached its peak and settled, shuddering as it did so. Bloody hell it was loud! And it moved by itself! We watched it slowly twist and shake its way across the room.

"Ok, Big Bertha," I said, "let's get you back in your corner." Every morning and evening I walked it back into its starting position, a minor inconvenience because Big Bertha gave us cool drinks whenever we wanted and that felt like real luxury. We stocked Bertha with food from a couple of shops in Claremont, a suburb of Perth not far from camp. Margaret loved pineapples and ate a lot of them, we would always have one or two in the fridge. Good old Bertha never let us down, but how we stood the noise I don't know, Dale slept in the same room as the fridge and he never once complained.

CHAPTER 20

Seeing double

I didn't really want to, but I went back to work for NuRoof after I was paid full wages for the job over in Kalgoorlie. I made sure I kept out of the way of the office staff; the four stolen ute wheels were never spoken of again. I was back on the local jobs and sometimes saw Sam at the yard where we managed to exchange a word or two. I was glad to see that his eye was healing well, and to hear that he had a few jobs lined-up, but none in the outback just yet. To me this meant he was back on-form and feeling okay. He invited Margaret, Dale and me to his home the next weekend that Margaret was free, I asked how Maureen would feel about it – knowing that Margaret wouldn't be too happy if I invited friends without asking her first - and Sam said she wanted us to come visit.

Sometimes, the ute that NuRoof allowed me to use outside of work needed to be repaired, which meant I had to walk from the train station to the yard where Richard and I would get picked up and taken by one of the chaps from the office out to a local job. After work one day I was walking down Hay Street back to the railway station when I decided to explore the shopping area called 'London Court'. I found the shops there very interesting, and one in particular caught my attention – a coin and stamp collector's shop. There were a couple of Gibsons stamp books in the window together with a notice that read 'We buy coins and stamps and albums – good prices paid, especially for those from Britain'. I was keen to find out more because I had brought my old Gibsons stamp books with me from Hull, and they contained some very old stamps, plenty from the UK and even from countries that had changed their name since the stamps were issued. I thought that if there was any value in the books, I would sell them to raise some money to add to our savings account.

I opened the shop door and did a double take at the sight of the man standing behind the counter. *I'm sure I've seen him before* I thought, *maybe he's got a double or I've seen his brother*, but in that moment, I couldn't place where I'd laid eyes on him. After some small talk I said I'd be back in a few days with the books to show him. I found out there was another dealer who also bought and sold stamps, and who came through town every few weeks on his rounds through a few towns and cities.

One of the alleyways in London Court

By the time I got home I had missed my steak and chips but wasn't bothered because Big Bertha had plenty of food waiting for me! I told Margaret the next time we were in town we'd take the stamp books and stroll down to London Court to find out if the books had any value.

Margaret was working the next few weekends and we didn't manage a trip into Perth as a family, so a week or so later I took the stamp books with me to work and visited the shop when my shift had finished. The second time I saw the stamp-dealer I was even more sure I'd either seen him before or he was related to the man I had seen – somewhere. Anyway, he took a look through the book and kept saying,

"Interesting! Interesting!" He seemed to keep flicking back to the same few pages.

"You can leave the book with me," he said, "I'll get the out-of-town dealer's advice on your collection." Then, it came to me, this was either the same man or the double of the man I worked with down in Albany, the one who made me feel so uncomfortable and who creeped me out so much I wanted to get away from him as fast as possible. Alarm bells rang inside my head.

"I'll come back when the other dealer is here and will show him myself," I replied.

His attitude changed. "Look, I know the book has some age to it, but the collection isn't worth very much." I noticed he kept flicking back to the same few pages again. Umming and aahing he added,

"Ok, look, I'll give you fifty dollars for the whole book, now." This made me dislike him even more – if he was prepared to give me that sort of money (a lot back then and the equivalent to about £400 in 2022) he had spotted something that was worth a lot more.

"No thanks, I'll call back when the dealer comes around again," and with that I grabbed my book and left the shop. I told Margaret about this adventure, and we never visited London Court again. I never did sell the stamp books; I couldn't bring myself to part with them.

Back at NuRoof 'my' ute had come out of the repair shop and once again I was independently mobile. Bruno was out of the hospital, had recovered from his spider bite and was back working at NuRoof. We teamed-up again and most of our work was local for a while. We were allocated another job at the Swan River Brewery, this time repairing the felt on a different part of the building and somewhere we hadn't previously explored. The brewery breaktime routine was exactly the same as last time – the hooter sounded several times a day for the workers to queue for their grog, but this time we didn't join the queue. I loved the views from the roof, they were spectacular, we could see along the river down to the Indian Ocean; it's a shame I didn't have my camera with me.

On Graylands I often went to check on how the new accommodation blocks were coming along, hoping they'd be ready in time for when our daughter (fingers crossed) was born, and that we'd be given the keys to one of the new flats. The truth was that no-one yet knew who would be lucky enough to get one. It's funny when you think about it: we'd left our two-up, two-down 'slum' house in Hull and travelled across the world to live in a big tin can in the blazing sunshine, and neither accommodation had their own indoor toilet and bathroom! We might have been in one of the new council houses by now if we had remained back in Hull, with our own bathroom and garden. But, we wouldn't have had all these experiences, I wouldn't have seen the view from the roof of Swan Brewery, and we wouldn't have tasted crayfish on a magical evening overlooking Perth. Mind you, we could have done without the spiders, ants and blazing heat all the time, but you don't get owt for nowt! This was an emotionally turbulent time for sure.

CHAPTER 21

We tremble, cracks open-up and a Margaret has an admirer

Then came along another experience we could have done without. Margaret and I were in the Nissen hut when all of a sudden everything began to vibrate and shake – even Big Bertha was moving more than usual. At first, we had no idea what was happening and clung on to whatever we could to stop it, and us, from falling. A few pots fell off the shelves and crashed onto the floor. The shaking and trembling lasted a few seconds but what a scary few seconds they were. When all was quiet again, we ventured outside and realised it must have been an earthquake.

At first, we thought everyone on camp was affected but then we saw that only the residents of the huts in a direct line with ours were outside looking dazed and puzzled. The huts outside this line were unaffected including those directly opposite our hut. The site manager came round to check on us all and everyone seemed to be all right, just a bit shaken-up by the experience. Margaret and I had a few sleepless nights after that worrying if it was going to happen again. I had no idea then that soon I would be coming across the place where the earthquake began.

Bruno and I were next given a job in the outback - this time only a few hundred miles outside Perth but far enough away that we needed to stay over in a hotel. There was a lot of talk in the yard and around camp about the earthquake and the damage it had caused in some places, but apart from a few broken pots we didn't see any damage as such; luckily, the accommodation blocks on camp weren't in the earthquake's path and were still standing.

On our way to the job in the outback and about fifty or so miles (80 kilometres) outside of Perth, we came across a massive crater right in the middle of the road. We concluded that this is where the earthquake began. My, what a sight it was! About 20 feet (six metres) wide and about 15 feet (four and a half metres) long, tapering to a narrower crack that seemed to stretch on for miles. There were a few makeshift signs stuck in the ground around the crater's widest part that read, 'Keep away! Find a way to continue your journey!'. The ute was rugged and robust enough that we could drive off the road into the scrub to make our way around the crater.

As we got nearer to our destination there were an increasing number of utes heading in the opposite direction, back towards the crater. The drivers and passengers were all shouting and bellowing with excitement as they drove past us. To me this was strange behaviour that I attributed to the effects of living in the blazing sunshine, although perhaps it was also because they lived in an outback town where nothing much ever happened. Whatever the reason, I didn't want my family to end-up whooping with excitement at the prospect of visiting a hole in the road! And the longer we stayed here, the more likely this outcome seemed.

The roofing job was easy and straightforward, but it was close to an Aborigine settlement, which meant we needed to be constantly vigilant, making sure we kept our tools, material and the ute safely in our sights at all times. Luckily, there was a secure storage place in the hotel's yard the manager said we could use, allowing us to relax after work and get a good night's sleep. I think if we'd lost another four wheels Alec might have spontaneously combusted, and that's a sight we didn't want to see!

In the town we saw a lot of Aborigine men and women hanging about in the streets, drunk and begging. Such a sorry sight they were. I don't know how Australia had developed like this, treating the native Australians so badly, their way of life had been destroyed, they had no future and no hope unless they adapted to the ways of the White Australians who were in control. It was very sad.

Bruno shook his head. "We do the job and get back home – quick as possible." I think all our nervousness worrying about our equipment gave us an energy boost and we finished the job in double-quick time. Before we knew it, we were back at the gaping crater, which by now had a fence erected around its widest part where dozens of people were snapping away with their cameras. I got chatting to a chap in what looked like a uniform (khaki-coloured shirt, shorts and hat) and he turned out to be the local ranger. He told me this was the biggest quake they'd ever had in this area, and that it caught a troop of kangaroos unawares, they'd hopped right in to the crater when the tremor struck directly along their regular route across this part of the outback. *Oh hell, I hope they didn't have any joeys with them*, I thought. I couldn't tell how deep the crack in the ground went but it was obvious there was no chance of climbing or hopping back out of it.

The weather was becoming more and more humid as the season rolled on from spring into summer; we'd passed through winter months ago, hardly noticing it except for some rain showers. Following the work with Bruno in the outback, I teamed-up with Richard on a local job in Claremont and one day when we finished work, I asked if he would like to come back to our home to meet Margaret and Dale (if he was around!) and have a cup of tea with us. He accepted and was pleased to have been asked.

We were chatting away the best we could when Richard said he was not very impressed with our living accommodation. He told us that when he and his parents arrived many years ago, they had rented a house hoping to save enough money to buy their own, but even after all these years they would never be able to afford to buy one. We all agreed that this wasn't the dream we were sold when encouraged to come over here to make a new life. Richard said that he and his family all wished they were back home in Poland. Most of the time I got the gist of what he said, but Richard's accent was very thick and sometimes I couldn't make out what he was saying. On this occasion though, it was very clear what he meant: I drove him back home and dropped him off at his door.

"Margaret is lovely woman, yes. Very attractive indeed! You are lucky man!" I liked the lad, but I didn't invite him back to our home again!

CHAPTER 22

Dale has admirers; Christmas is nigh and a dam visit

One weekend, Sam and his two girls called at our hut and Sam asked if I was interested in some more work in the outback.

"I'm waiting until after our baby daughter is born," crossing my fingers when I said 'baby daughter'. Sam went on to tell me that he had finished with NuRoof again and was doing some contracting work with another firm near Coolgardie. Sam's older daughter asked where Dale was – of course he was out with his mates as usual.

"Let's go and find him," I said, thinking they'd be in their den. The four of us went for a walk around the camp passing the new accommodation blocks on the way. Sam was impressed with the buildings' progress.

"You're bound to get one of those, Yorkie, what with a baby on the way and a growing lad already!" I hoped he was right. We reached the den and found Dale and his mates inside,

"How are you doing, lads?" I asked.

Dale stuck his head out of the den's doorway, "Ok, dad!"

"These lasses want to look around your den, so budge-up and make space for them, lads." I said, knowing that Dale and his mates didn't really want any girls in their den, but out of forced politeness they shuffled-up to make some room. Sam gave them some good tips on how to make their den stronger, and they listened eagerly to him.

"You need a sign outside saying, 'Boys Only, NO Girls!'" The lads all grinned and nodded but Sam's girls scowled at him. When it was time to leave Sam turned to me.

"Don't forget, Yorkie, if you want any help at all you know where we live, and don't forget about the outback work coming up. Let me know when you're ready."

"Aye, ok Cockney, I'll do that!" I replied shaking his hand.

We were now about two months away from our second Christmas down under, and we decided to buy ourselves a television that we'd seen advertised on one of the camp's noticeboards. Yet another family was moving away and selling all their surplus possessions. The tv was black-and-white with its own indoor aerial that we had to twist and turn into just the right configuration when the tv was in a specific position in the room. The tv helped make the long evenings feel shorter – remember, even in summer it got dark quite early in Australia - although all the programmes were at least two years behind what we'd already seen back in Old Blighty. We now had Big Bertha slowly and noisily dancing across the room, and our very own goggle-box turning our little hut into a 'high-tech' home.

Over in the UK it was late autumn; Elsie continued to regularly send us letters, photos and newspaper cuttings of items of local interest either in Hull or the surrounding villages like Hutton Cranswick. I remember one photo of the very tall horse chestnut trees in their full autumn glory around the scenic village pond. I stared at that photo a lot and thought I could make out some big conkers dangling from the thick, strong branches. Sometimes, I imagined myself sitting on the bench overlooking the pond. Oh well, I was sure I'd return there one day to collect conkers with Dale and his sister.

Margaret, Dale and me, we continued to go on regular trips into Perth to have a good look around the city and its shops, and this time we needed some Christmas cards. Mooching through one of the malls I spotted the bugger who gave me the window cleaning job, and who didn't pay me my full wages after the cleaning equipment and ladder were pinched from the front of the shop. He was cleaning the windows himself and he spotted me. We glared at each other.

On we strolled to a café to enjoy some iced tea sitting in the shade of the mall's canopy. It was at times like this that I wondered if we were doing the right thing thinking of returning to the UK. Margaret and I had been discussing it a lot lately and had decided to return home to England. We couldn't see how we would ever afford our own house, and we didn't want to live permanently with me working in the outback for weeks on end. The doubts about staying were few and far between, and most of the time we knew that going back to Blighty was the right thing for us to do.

I was thankful we had use of the work's ute to get out and about on our time off, but sometimes Dale wanted a change and so we ventured out on the train. One time we travelled from Claremont to Perth, then by a local bus to wherever it was going to see what was going on in another suburb. What a disaster that was! We reached the terminus and decided to make our way back to a small, covered shopping area. There was no-one around, probably because it was around midday and the temperature was peaking. We later learnt that it was common for people in the suburbs to have a siesta. Luckily, we found a shop selling cool drinks; there was nothing else to see nor do there so we waited for an hour before catching the next bus back to Perth.

As usual I kept a regular eye on the camp's noticeboards and one day spotted an advertisement for a coach trip to one of the local reservoirs called Serpentine Pipehead Dam reservoir. Luckily, the day of the outing fell on Margaret's next work-free weekend, I went to the camp's office and booked three tickets for us, returning home excited to tell Margaret and Dale. The dam wasn't far out of Perth, about a 90-minutes' drive, which was about 45 miles (72 kilometres) by the time everyone was picked up – the coach made several stops in addition to the camp. There were a few other Graylands Poms on the coach and we were all in a jolly mood because the coach was air-conditioned and kept us nice and cool.

When we parked-up at our destination, Dale and I were keen to go on the guided tour but Margaret wanted to stay behind on the coach to keep out of the heat. The guide told us that the dam was opened in 1961 and was one of the main water supplies for Perth. Construction of the reservoirs and dams around Perth was proposed in 1887, and before then most people relied on shallow wells fed from rainwater tanks. The guide also said that the water level of the reservoir had been getting lower and lower over recent years, and that it hadn't reached its maximum level for many years.

The dam and reservoir were impressive feats of engineering built on a plateau covered in open woodland. Dale and I enjoyed walking around with the guide, taking snaps with my Kodak camera and exploring a few of the short paths around the dam. Margaret didn't see much of the dam but she said she was happy enough keeping cool in the coach, so all-in-all it was another good day out for our family.

Dale above Serpentine Pipehead Dam reservoir and off camera to the right-hand side is Serpentine Dam itself.

CHAPTER 23

A corrupt cop keeps the law in these parts

It was a couple of weeks since Sam and his girls had been to visit us and then he got back in touch about a job not too far away from Perth. Far enough for us to stay away, but it wouldn't take long he said, and he was keen for me to join him because he needed someone 'with experience of the outback'. Work at NuRoof was a bit slack in the few weeks before Christmas, and sometimes we spent our days tidying-up around the yard. On top of that, I didn't have use of the ute at the weekends for a while, so there was no reason not to go along with Sam for a few days, after all, it would be more money towards our fare home. Margaret wasn't very happy about it but agreed we could make good use of the extra money.

Sam told me he had worked that area before, that it was near an Aborigine settlement, and it was one we didn't want to hang around in. He also said he would do 'all the talking'. I had no idea what he meant at that point but said,

"That's fine with me, Cockney!" All I knew was that the job was to replace some corrugated sheeting, and that we would need to keep an eye on all our equipment again.

We drove about 200 miles (320 kilometres) from Perth when we came to a railway crossing in an area covered with gum trees that were stripped of their bark. Several other dust tracks branched off in all directions. Sam slowed the ute to a crawl.

"Here he comes. Don't say a word, Yorkie!" With that, a huge ute appeared out of nowhere kicking-up dust and pulled in front of us, and out climbed a sheriff of the law. What a sight he was: bandy legs overhung by a big beer-belly, a big hat on his bonce and an even bigger swagger as he made his way over to us.

"G'day mate," he said to Sam, "where're you heading, and how long you gonna be in this area?" I was getting a bit nervous by now, but Sam didn't blink.

"G'day Sheriff! We've met before. We're doing a job over in the town and will be around for a week at the most."

"Well," the sheriff replied, "if we've met before you'll know what I can do for in-comers like you fellas around here. You'll know I make sure you're safe in town being so close to that Aborigine settlement over there, and you'll know I keep everything nice and peaceful around here for everybody!" *Blimey!* I thought, *Are we in a spaghetti western?* Then he looked across at me and back at Sam.

"Is this your mate?"

"Yes, Yorkie's been with me a while now and he's good – everything's ok there!" Sam reached out of the ute's open window to shake the sheriff's hand and I caught a glimpse of a 10 dollar note, the equivalent of about 80 English pounds today (2022).

"When you've finished the job and you're on your way back, drive straight through – no need to stop." Sam nodded and we continued on our way.

"Is it always like this over in this area?" I asked.

"I don't know what you mean, Yorkie!" replied Sam grinning. "Sometimes the handshake is a crate of grog. It's worth it though because he does keep things quiet round here." Perhaps we wouldn't need to worry about our material and equipment now we were 'friends' with the local sheriff.

The job itself was another easy one and the accommodation was 'first-class' again by virtue of the public phone in the hotel lobby. Sam called his family every night and told Maureen we'd be home by the weekend. We were getting on with the work so well that mid-week we took the afternoon off and went target-practising with Sam's air rifle, driving away from the town in the opposite direction to where we met the sheriff. We bumped along the dusty tracks looking for a suitable place to stop when I pointed out the blue lake shimmering in the distance. Sam said we'd carry on and drive right through it, he'd experienced many of these mirages before but it was my first chance to see one this close-up. The closer we got to the blue expanse of 'water' the stranger the experience was: my brain thought we were about to drive into a transparent lake - I could see right through to the other side of it, then when we got close enough the lake became dust and sand. We continued driving through it and watched the lake disappear around us until we reached the other side, turning around there it was again! Very strange.

Eventually, we came across a clump of gum trees that formed an area good for target-practice and were about to unload when we spotted a troop of kangaroo heads bobbing along over the brow of the hillock. We knew the sound of the air rifle would carry some distance through this landscape and it might spook the kangaroos so we didn't fire a single shot that day.

That evening back at the hotel bar when Sam and I were enjoying our nightly grog or two, who should stride in but the sheriff. He picked up a large glass of lager from the bar – not sure if he paid for it – and made a beeline for us.

"G'day fellas!" he said, sitting on the bench opposite ours. Sam turned to me and nodded which meant 'keep quiet, Yorkie'.

"Now my Pommie mates, how has your day been? Did you enjoy your drive? How was your shooting-practice?" He was telling us he knew every move we made over here. Sam took it all in his stride.

"We went driving to show Yorkie here what a mirage is – it's his first one up-close." He was about to continue when two big blokes loudly burst through the hotel door singing at the top of their voices and made straight for the bar. The sheriff turned around and stood-up.

"Fellas, fellas, keep the noise down over there!" Then he turned back to us and said, "no worries with the boys, there, they're cattle drovers letting off a bit of steam, they won't cause trouble while I'm around!" The two blokes at the bar were quiet now, took their grogs and shuffled over to a corner table, heads down.

"I'm going to have a quiet word with them fellas," he said making his way over to their table. The cattle drovers stuck out their hands for the sheriff to shake and I could just make out a flash of colour of five-dollar notes exchanged between palms. The sheriff smiled at the men. "Get them horses cleaned and take good care of 'em!" They looked up at him and nodded, touching their fingers to their hats.

The sheriff came back over to us and before I could stop myself, I blurted out.

"What an interesting country you live in!" Sam looked at me and winked, a big smile spread across the sheriff's face and he began to laugh so hard it made his belly wobble.

"I'll be back to see you two fellas before you leave – don't worry, I'll know where you are!" And with that he left, laughing and wobbling as he went.

"Good on yer, Yorkie!" Sam said grinning, "you said the right thing there!"

"Ooph! I was dreading him holding out his hand for me to shake. If he had, I would have spent the night behind bars for sure!" Sam burst out laughing.

"Keep it down, Cockney, we don't want him coming back!" I urged, but that made him laugh more which set me off. After a few minutes we calmed down and I asked,

"What I want to know, is how does he know where we were and what we were doing?"

"You know we're close to an Aborigine settlement? We're in their territory, or it used to be theirs and they still keep a close watch on it. Anything that happens here, they know about, and report back to the sheriff. He looks after them in return." I was still puzzled.

"But we didn't see anyone all the time we were out there?"

"No," Sam said, "but they were watching us, all the time." I squirmed in my seat, uneasy at the thought of being watched, Sam noticed my reaction.

"Don't worry, Yorkie, we'll stay well clear of their settlement."

A day or so later we finished the job. There was no need to tidy-up and remove the leftover scraps because we knew that some of the Aborigine chaps would come over and take everything back to their place to use in some way, nothing went to waste out here. We had a couple of roofing sheets left.

"What about these?" I asked, "What should I do with them?"

110

"It's ok, Yorkie, load them up, I've got this covered." I didn't know what Sam meant but loaded them onto the ute as instructed.

"We've got a drop-off on our way back" he added. Sure enough, about 10 miles (16 kilometres) into our drive back home – with no lawman in sight - we pulled off the main track onto a smaller, dusty track and headed toward a smallholding. The sound of barking dogs filled the air; before I had time to wonder what would happen next, Sam stopped the ute, jumped out and walked toward a giant of a man who appeared from one of the outbuildings. They shook hands and by now I knew what that meant. While I was busy looking at the poor state of some of the roofs on the outbuildings – rusty with more holes than metal - the two sheets I'd put on the ute had been whipped off the back and were heading towards the sheds. Exchange completed, Sam jumped back in the ute and away we drove.

About a mile or so later he handed me a 10 dollar note.

"Yorkie, take this. We were never going to pay the sheriff out of our own money – *we* weren't going to pay to do the work! What we just got is twice what we paid the lawman." He went on to tell me that the giant man had an outbuilding full of stuff that was added to, and taken from, by truckers passing along the same route we'd travelled. I wondered if the sheriff knew about this, he must have done and allowed it to go on? Somehow everyone benefitted out here.

"Well," I said, "at least now he can repair his roof." Sam turned to me with a glint in his good eye – the damaged one was still healing.

"Yorkie, why would he repair his rotten roof when he hasn't seen any rain for months? Plus, he's got a bore hole to give him drinking water and he doesn't need to collect rain from a roof." Then it dawned on me: he kept all those dogs to protect the gear he was buying and selling.

I suddenly felt as green as I had been the first time I worked with Sam on a job in the outback. We drove the rest of the way to Perth in silence. I was thinking over the experiences of the last week and how Sam had adapted to the Aussie way of doing things in the outback, and I knew I couldn't. There was no way Margaret would stand for any of the hand-shake dealings even if I was okay with it, which I wasn't. No, if surviving

111

over here meant living like this, then it wasn't for me and my family. In that moment, I knew the right thing for me and my family was to return to Good Old Blighty.

CHAPTER 24

Some good news and a trip to Scarborough

Sam dropped me off at Graylands and we arranged to go to the beach the following weekend, one that Margaret, Dale and I hadn't visited before. There was a buzz in the air on camp with a rumour circulating about the tin Nissen huts and how they would soon all be replaced by brick-built accommodation, which meant everyone would eventually get their own apartment. About time too, although we had got used to ours and found it cosy in its own way. Then we received the good news that we were one of the first families allocated an apartment in the new accommodation block. All we had to do now was wait for it to be finished, which couldn't be too far off. That news cheered us up no end and hopefully, we would be in there before our daughter was born (yes, still keeping my fingers crossed!)

As arranged, Sam called at the weekend to pick us up and take both families to the beach, this one was called 'Scarborough Beach' about a forty minutes' drive from Graylands. It couldn't have looked less like our beloved Yorkshire Scarborough beach: pale, golden sands that seemed to stretch on for miles lapped by greeny-blue clear water edged with snowy-white, gentle breakers. The wide beach was dotted with tall trees and manmade canopies to provide some shade from the sun. We found a sheltered spot, set-up Sam's four deckchairs and spread out the picnic blanket.

There was a wooden cabin close by selling cold, soft drinks and straightaway, the three kids made a beeline for it. Dale would never admit it, but I could see he was loving all the attention he got from Sam's two girls. There were plenty of lifeguards on duty stationed every few yards down the beach, which meant we didn't worry about the kids going-off on their own adventure down the beach, even though we knew there were Great White Sharks (the kind that find humans tasty) in this stretch of water. The lifeguards were on the lookout for them and were ready to sound a loud horn-blast, calling everyone out of the sea. Dale and the girls knew about this and were under strict instructions to stay close to the beach when they went into the water. Dale was enjoying learning to surf and was showing off to the girls, although whenever I was watching them, I saw him fall over.

Sam and Maureen told us they had had to get their house sprayed for an infestation of black-clocks (big, black cockroaches). They hid in every nook and cranny of the house and it took specialist treatment to get rid of them, like it did when the spiders invaded the huts on camp. Sharks and insects notwithstanding, we had a smashing day, what with good company, a lovely spot on the beach and a refreshing breeze to keep the temperature bearable. Margaret was feeling relaxed too, although the heat was getting to her more than ever. When Sam dropped us back at Graylands he said he would come and pick us up in a few weeks on Christmas Day and we'd all go to the beach taking our Christmas fare with us, in traditional Aussie style!

CHAPTER 25

Christmas Australian style!

The next few weeks leading-up to Christmas were pretty low-key: I was back with NuRoof again working on a few local jobs; and there was no festive buzz in the air like there would be over in Britain at this time of year. I got to thinking about all the shops in the centre of Hull with their decorated windows, the coloured lights hung across Whitefriargate and the Salvation Army Band playing in the square in front of City Hall. All being well my football team – Hull City – would be playing on Boxing Day, and I thought *This time next year Dale and I will be watching them play.* Me and a few mates on camp tried to arrange our own football match for Boxing Day but there wasn't much take-up due to the rising summer temperatures.

We received loads of cards from back home and added them to the Christmas decorations around the hut to make it look more festive. We had posted our cards back to the UK weeks ago to make sure they arrived in time for the Big Day. The weekend before the 25th the three of us took a trip into Perth to buy a few more presents such as a bigger surfboard for Dale – he would need it to show off to Sam's girls on Christmas Day at the beach. I showed them where I had worked for a few weeks with Taffy on the big, city centre tower blocks, they were nearly finished and ready for the V.I.P. Ambassadors to move in. Dale seemed impressed that his very own dad had helped build them. Then for some reason I had a thought, when our daughter is born, she'll be a Perthie – someone from Perth, and the rest of us are Yorkies. I told Dale he will soon have a Perthie sister.

"Ok, dad," he said. I think he hid his excitement very well! Dale had turned nine a week ago and probably wasn't interested in a baby brother or sister, now he was all 'grown-up'.

In the week before Christmas, there was no work at NuRoof, the jobs had dried-up. I didn't mind because it gave me a few more days off to spend with Dale and Margaret when she wasn't working. One day I went looking for Dale around the camp and came across a large skip full of stuff people wanted rid of. I saw a large folder held together with Sellotape and I couldn't leave it there without first taking a look inside. Carefully, I unfastened the tape and opened the folder to find a redddish/orange/pinkish picture of what looked like native Aborigine artwork. The picture showed a cave entrance with walls covered in drawings of kangaroos, boomerangs and men throwing their boomerangs. I loved it, even though parts of it were torn. Someone had liked it enough to repair it with Sellotape and I knew it was coming home with me. Margaret wasn't impressed of course.

The picture I salvaged from a skip. It depicts the story of the boomerang, described in the attached clipping as an 'Australian Aborigine Legend'. The orange/brown stripes are the original strips of Sellotape still holding the picture together!

"You should have left it in the skip, throw it away!" she said, but I didn't, and I still have it today. In fact, it's in a frame hung on the wall of my hobby room, and do you know what, the original Sellotape is still holding it together!

Just before Christmas day, Dale told me he and his mates wanted to build a new den, one made of bricks. When I asked where they would get the bricks from, Dale said they would show me, so off we went across the camp to the building-site of the new accommodation blocks. The workmen had all knocked-off for a few days over the Christmas holidays and the site was unguarded, Dale, his mates and I had it all to ourselves. The building site was like an adventure playground, it even had a brick hoist – a platform to winch a load of bricks off the ground up to the level where they were needed.

"Climb aboard, lads!" I said, waving them over to the platform. I pulled on the winch and slowly raised them up into the air. "Take a good look around to see where you want your next den!" I shouted up at them. The boys agreed on a spot and pointed at a clump of under-growth just on the edge of the building-site. We spent the rest of the morning hefting bricks from their neatly stacked pile over to the spot for the lads' new den.

I showed them how to lay them, one layer at a time and left them to build their new den. I suppose I wasn't being very responsible, but I felt good showing them how to do something. I didn't have much of an education myself and when I could pass on to Dale some form of my own learning, I tried my best. Who knows, maybe those adventures he had with his mates building dens and playing around on a building site sparked his interest in building and making things, and helped make him the clever chap he is today. I like to think so.

Christmas Day finally arrived and with it, Sam in his ute to collect me and Dale, and Maureen and the girls in their car to collect Margaret and all of our festive food. There were too many people and too much food to squeeze into one vehicle. Away we all went back to Scarborough Beach for the day. For us Poms it was a very different way to spend Christmas Day but we enjoyed it. Dale tried out his new surfboard and made the girls laugh whether he meant to or not. I could stand upright on it for a few minutes, but Sam was the star of the show and was in his element showing-off his surfing skills.

I really enjoyed swimming in the clear, blue-green water of the Indian Ocean, what a relief it was from the heat of the summer sun. Margaret stayed in the shade of Sam and Maureen's big umbrellas and said she felt a bit wobbly. She was much bigger with this baby than she had been with Dale, and this late in the pregnancy found everything really difficult, even bending down. I kept a close eye on her as did Maureen. In our first few months over here, Margaret had got badly burned at Cottesloe Beach and ended up with large blisters on her back and a touch of sunstroke. We were all a bit more savvy now and made sure we were in the shade or covered-up in the midday sun. As the day wore on, the beach got more crowded and we eventually decided it was time to leave. Sam and Maureen took us all back to their house where we played a few board games to finish-off a memorable and very enjoyable Christmas Day.

We spent Boxing Day with Margaret's boss and family at their bungalow. Dale loved it there, spending most of his time in their swimming pool. During the meal the conversation turned to the price of land and houses around Perth, and Bill agreed that they were out of reach for most ordinary working families. He went on to ask us what we wanted our futures to be over there. That's when we felt a bit awkward because we hadn't told anybody that we were going to go to the travel agents and book our passage back to Britain and had even decided on a date of arrival - by October 1969. I can't remember what we said exactly, perhaps something a bit vague. Knowing Bill and his wife, they probably sensed we were thinking about returning home to England. Before long, another lovely day came to an end – thank you Bill and your Perthie family for giving us such nice memories!

To complete the 1968 Christmas festivities a few days later we were enjoying a meal with Carol and Neville at their home. I think they cooked a traditional meal and even had crackers to pull at the heavily laden table. Carol said it was a tradition her parents had brought with them from Britain and that she continued with it. We said that one day she should go to Hull to see where her parents came from, and this made me wonder if our Perthie daughter would ever want to come back to see where she was born.

CHAPTER 26

January 1969 – Moving day at last!

With the festive fun over it was time to return to work, Margaret to her light duties at the hospital and me to whatever local jobs were trickling in at NuRoof. Sam appeared one day and asked if I wanted another job in the outback but I turned him down, it was too close to Margaret's due date at the end of the month. I was getting very nervous now watching poor Margaret struggle with the summer temperatures that climbed to well over 100°F (38 to 40°C) during the day and only dropped to around 80°F (27°C) at night. The news reported that summer as a 'real scorcher' that had already broken many records.

I told Margaret I thought it was time she stopped working but stubborn as ever, she refused, wanting to continue for as long as possible to maintain our income. One weekend, she was brought home from work after fainting and was diagnosed with heatstroke. Another time when she felt very hot and sick, we went to the hospital and she was given antibiotics to control a mild infection. Even Dale must have begun to worry because he curtailed his wanderings and stayed closer to home. Although, there was another reason for this change: I found out that when the site manager returned to work after the Christmas holiday and found Dale and his mates had moved a load of bricks and used them to build a den, he gave them a good rollocking and told them to put them all back. I think that brought the gang's adventures to an end for a while, and they decided to lay low until the incident was forgotten.

The tension caused by the heat and pregnancy was eased a bit when we received a couple of letters and read the exciting news that my nephew, Brian - a Royal Navy man, was sailing along the Australian coast and had requested a transfer to another vessel that would be docking at Fremantle in late February to early March. The second letter confirmed his permission to transfer. Yes! We would be welcoming our first visitor from Britain! What a feeling that was, like bringing a part of our 'real' home closer to us and making the dream of returning to our beloved Blighty feel possible.

We were so excited about Brian's visit that we told our friends on Graylands, they were pleased for us and said they wanted to meet him. Gerry and Lil invited us to bring Brian along to one of our regular get-togethers; these involved their youngest daughter, Kathy (about 10 years old) singing a medley of pop songs such as *Ferry Across the Mersey* and *Lily the Pink*, and some Beatle's classics: *A Hard Day's Night,* and *She Loves You*. My, could she belt out those songs for such a young 'un! Gerry, his son, Dale and me, we formed a backing group bashing some spoons on tin cans to accompany Kathy, but what a racket we must have made! It was fun though, and gave us dads the chance to share a few bevvies while the mums enjoyed a good chat.

We had come to know a lot of immigrants from the UK and several of them came to visit us at this time, maybe they were excited about the soon-to-be-born baby and were keeping an eye on Margaret. That's what it felt like – we were looking out for each other, and I was thankful for that when I was at work and away from Margaret, even though I was only working in Perth.

One of the local jobs was at Perth Railway Goods Yard repairing shed roofs. The work was easy but there were too many scorpions and too much heat! By midday me and my mate, we knocked-off to find some shade in the goods waggons and got our heads down for a siesta until it was time to report back at the yard. Mind you, that was only after we had located the scorpion nest and burnt it out of the waggon! It's funny how doing this felt almost normal now. I had the personal use of a ute again and was grateful for that because although our weekend outings had stopped – Margaret couldn't bear the heat by now – it meant that when the time came, I could get her to the hospital, quick.

The day finally came when we received notice that our new accommodation would be ready within the week, some of our friends were also moving into the new apartment block. It was all very exciting, and even more so when we received a letter from a shipping company in Fremantle about our worldly goods - that we'd packed into crates back in Hull eighteen months ago – they were ready to collect from storage. Good old Sam and Maureen said they would collect and store our crates at their place, and our Graylands friends offered help in moving them into our new flat.

The feeling of friendship, all pulling together and helping each other was great. I know I haven't experienced anything like it in the years since we returned to Britain, at least not on the same scale. As well as all the new towns, terrain, landmarks, animals and plants we got to see in Australia, it's all the new people we met who made this time special for us. I hope many of them felt the same way, that our family helped to make their experiences in Australia special too.

It didn't matter where we were from in the UK or Europe, to the Australians we were all 'POMs' - 'Prisoners of Mother England'. I think that was annoying for the non-English UK immigrants, to suddenly be lumped together with the English and identified as such. Away from the Australians and together on camp we recognised these differences of course, making friends and connections across the UK while remaining within the bounds of the camp. For example, Kitty and her husband were from Ireland and had lived on Graylands longer than us. In all the time we were there we never met the husband who had gone to work in the mines in Dampier - about 950 miles (1530 kilometres) north of Perth – where he could earn bigger dollars. He and Kitty were saving-up to buy some land and a smallholding in Ireland. Kitty used to tell us lots of funny and sad yarns of life back in Ireland, which I soaked-up like a sponge because my dad was from the same county and I never got a chance to learn much about his early life. He abandoned my mam, my five sisters and me when I was about five. He ran away to Scotland to live with another woman, but that's another story!

Moving day came at last. We collected the key from the main office on camp and explored our new home, a dream come true with our very own bathroom! No more traipsing across to the communal shower and toilet blocks. Dale had his own bedroom, no more sleeping on the living room settee for him! Our new baby would begin her life in a safe home, not a tin hut we shared with spiders and ants. Me, Sam, and a few friends moved our boxes and crates from Sam's place to ours; somehow, we managed to relocate the walking, talking fridge Big Bertha into her new home, securing her firmly in place in the new kitchen.

Around the same time our friends were also moving into their new flats, and we all chipped in and helped each other shift boxes, crates, bits of furniture – anything and everything! Margaret and the lasses unpacked boxes and kept everyone fed and watered, while the kids 'helped' by keeping out of the way until it was time to unpack their own possessions in their new bedrooms. We must have celebrated after it was all done, although we were probably too tired by the end of the day. Tired, but very happy indeed.

CHAPTER 27

I make the biggest mistake of my life followed by the second biggest, and then a new day Dawns

Margaret was now about a fortnight away from her due date when a week's work in the outback came-up at NuRoof. No-one stepped forward even when the bosses increased the pay; before I knew what I was doing I volunteered. Of course, Margaret wasn't very happy about it, but I promised it was only for one week and would be the last outback job for a while, adding that the money would come in handy because we didn't know how long she would be off work. Reluctantly, she agreed and I committed myself to the work.

The plan was to pick-up a new Polish worker on the Sunday of the coming weekend. By the Saturday Margaret was feeling a bit restless so I went round to Gerry and Lil's and told them about the situation. They said they'd look after Dale, that he could go and stay with them and they'd make sure he went to school. By 9am on the Sunday morning Margaret was very uncomfortable and asked to be taken to the hospital. I popped over to Gerry and Lil's with Dale and left him there with a bag of his clothes, and of course his knife, fork and spoon. Then I whisked Margaret to Perth Hospital taking a shortcut across some dusty, bumpy tracks, Margaret showed her appreciation by colourfully cursing me!

On arrival at the hospital's Emergency Department entrance, I jumped out of the ute and rushed inside to look for a doctor or nurse. Within a few minutes Margaret was on a trolley, and about to be wheeled away when I just managed to give her a quick kiss; then she was gone – taken along to the labour ward. If I could go back and relive this time again I would do it differently; at the time I had committed to a job, we needed the money, a new workmate was waiting for me to pick him up, Dale was being well looked after and Margaret was in safe hands. What was the good of me cancelling the job and waiting around, I was useless, wasn't I? That's how I saw the situation at the time.

I was late picking-up my new workmate, and after he loaded his massive holdall in the back of the ute and climbed into the passenger seat, I explained the reason for being late.

"Tonight, we – how to say in English? 'Drink to wet the baby's head!'" He said in broken English. I shook my head because I didn't know if the baby was born yet and felt so tense and moody that I wasn't ready to celebrate. I kept thinking of Margaret on her own in the hospital and then pictured our Grayland friends and knew they would visit her. I couldn't relax though, and felt irritated, which wasn't helped by the problems my new workmate, Jan and I were having trying to understand one another. He couldn't speak much English and of course I didn't speak any Polish. It was an awkward and tense drive to our destination.

Luckily, the roofing job was going to be straightforward: no felt needed removing, we just needed to trim the edges where they had bubbled and flaked, sweep it down good and proper then add a couple of thick layers on top. Jan knew what he was doing and didn't need much instruction from me, but even so, I was in a bad mood for the first few days. I felt 'all wrong' leaving Margaret and being away like this, was the baby born by now? Do I have a baby son or a baby daughter? I was angry with myself for leaving her, for leaving Dale and for not being there for our new baby when she(?) appeared.

As the week wore on, we did 'wet the baby's head' (more in hope than certainty) and Jan paid for our grogs. He brought out a fist full of dollars from his wallet and was quick to knock back the booze but he, well neither of us, got drunk because the beer wasn't very strong. We drank it to quench our thirst after a day's work and to relax a bit in the evening, before embarking on the same routine the following day. On about day three of our week's work the ute stalled when we were driving from the hotel to the worksite.

"I fix it!" said Jan, jumping out of the ute and picking-up a small, blue hammer from the toolbox in the back. He lifted the bonnet and started shouting in Polish, probably swearing his head off. He began tapping at the engine with the hammer then signalled to me to turn the key – nothing. We repeated this several times, each hammer-blow increasingly harder, Jan's shouting louder and fiercer until 'Whack!' one mighty crack of the hammer, a key turned, and the ute spluttered into life.

"Car-bur-retor, is choked-up," he said, "ute needs service." After that incident we seemed to get on better, although in reality maybe I began to relax a bit because I knew he was a good worker and could help get us out of a fix. His skills with the hammer were second-to-none and whenever the engine stopped, we got it going again. Well, most of the time.

We were close to finishing the job when I said if we made an early start the following day, we could get it done and set-off back to Perth driving through the night to reach home a day earlier than expected. Jan agreed and the next day we made good progress, finishing before the hottest part of the day. We decided to take a rest before setting-off at sundown to drive through the night when it was cooler. I was excited at the thought I'd soon be back with Margaret, Dale and our new addition to the family – all being well. We set off and the ute was going along fine for about an hour when it began to cough and splutter, coming to a halt with one mighty shudder. Jan looked over at me.

"Hammer!" he said, but this time no amount of bashing would bring the engine back to life.

"Don't worry, Jan there'll soon be another ute or truck passing this way, and they'll give us a tow.' Even before I had finished the sentence, I knew I was talking rubbish. There was no chance any other vehicle would be along this small, dusty track during the night – we would have to sit and wait it out until someone came along in the morning.

The night sky was peppered with stars and maybe I spotted a planet or two and a few shooting stars. There was no light pollution from towns or cities to impede the illumination from the heavenly bodies, which was spectacular. I would have enjoyed and appreciated it a lot more if I hadn't begun to feel very nervous.

We climbed back into the ute and Jan started to sing in Polish, maybe to steady his own nerves; I joined in with my version of *My Bonny Yorkshire Lass* and for a while we sat there harmonising until sitting in the ute became too uncomfortable. Next, we climbed back out and cleared an area of ground and spread a piece of cloth sheeting down on the ground, sitting ourselves on that with our backs resting against the ute. The temperature was dropping fast so we poured some liquid bitumen just in front of the sheet and set it alight.

The moon shone bright against the black, speckled sky and helped to keep our small, safe oasis visible. By now, Jan was singing at the top of his voice to keep snakes and any other creatures that came out at night looking for food away from us. I asked him what the song meant, and Jan replied that it was a Polish love song. I don't know if he had any family waiting for him in Perth, that night we preferred to sing our own songs rather than talk. Eventually, we ran out of steam for singing.

"How much water do we have left?" I asked.

"No worry, look in big bag, here," he said, holding open the mouth of the large holdall revealing half a dozen bottles of water and even more small bottles of grog. We cracked open a bottle each and guzzled them down.

As the night wore on the beer helped to calm our nerves but also made us more emotional. At one point, I got a very strange feeling of being alone and wondered if that's how Margaret felt when I left her at the hospital. That was a mistake for sure, but it was too late now to change it. Then a flurry of noises – difficult to make out what they were but they didn't sound friendly. I jumped up and found a piece of steel scrap in the back of the ute and started banging it with the hammer.

"Look!" said Jan pointing at the front of the ute where the silhouettes of a family of kangaroos were made visible by the moonlight. They turned, caught us staring at them and hopped away into the dark distance.

"Jan, what's that? Can you hear it? Whispering! Who is whispering?" It reminded me of some Aborigine sounds I heard in other places in the outback, and I remember Sam telling me we were always being watched, but did that mean everywhere in the outback? I don't know if I felt more or less afraid at the thought of being found by Aborigine people – would they hurt us, help us, or just want what we had in the ute? Before I had time to think what to do, Jan began to snore. I nudged him awake and he started whistling a bright, chirpy tune. I joined in, singing *Show Me the Way to Go Home* and *There'll Always Be an England*. Blimey, could Jan whistle and loud too! A man of many talents! The music we made can't have been to the liking of our Aborigine visitors because there was no more whispering after that.

The night dragged-on and we drank more grogs and a few bottles of water, being careful to leave plenty for the day ahead, when daylight would eventually arrive. Maybe it was the beer that helped us have the idea of putting on our work clothing. The overalls stank of bitumen and we thought the strong smell might keep away the scorpions, spiders and snakes. Perhaps too many beers and too many emotions overwhelmed our systems to the point we could no longer keep awake and we dozed-off.

Suddenly, I was startled awake by Jan screaming and shouting as he smashed a small snake to smithereens before it could slither any closer to us. Just as suddenly, I felt very calm and at peace, my night-fear fell away and I watched the sun peeking over the horizon bathing the land in golden, orange-coloured rays. In that moment, I knew Margaret and our new baby daughter were okay, and I knew her name too – Dawn!

In the distance I saw a dust trail, dust kicked-up by a vehicle's wheels.

"Look, Jan, look!" We waved our arms to attract the driver's attention but there was no need, he had already seen us and was heading our way. He slowed down and eventually stopped by our ute and makeshift encampment. A huge fellow wearing a rancher-style uniform headed towards us.

"G'day!" he said. "What happened here?" I explained the events of the previous evening, and he wasn't impressed. I heard him mutter to himself.

"Ya stupid Pommie bastards, will you never learn?" To our faces he said, "S'pose you want a tow into town? Ya can't leave the ute here fellas, or she'll be gone at worst, stripped clean at best." He and Jan busied themselves hitching the ute to the rancher's truck. We were just about to leave when I spotted our trusty blue hammer lying in the red dust. I picked it up and decided to claim it, and to this day it's safely stored in my toolbox.

The rancher stopped at a small hamlet and unhitched the ute.

"In a few days one of you Poms will be through this way. He's good with engines," he said, before wandering off towards the bar. There was no way we were hanging around here longer than we needed to. We followed the rancher to the bar-cum-hotel and found a phone. A few minutes later I got through to NuRoof and explained what had happened. They told me to phone back later and they would have sorted something out. I told them we weren't hanging around here, and if a truck was heading into Perth we'd catch a lift back leaving the ute in the hamlet if the trucker wouldn't tow it.

Luck was on our side and it wasn't long before a truck pulled-up outside the bar; the driver – after we bought him a few grogs at the bar and offered some more bottles to take away – agreed to take us and the ute with him to Perth. He said he knew a good garage in Perth and would drop us there. When Jan and I secured the ute to the truck, we noticed about half of our tools were missing from the box in the back. Those whisperings in the night were real! If our Aborigine visitors had been capable of lifting the ute and carrying it away, we would have been in big, big trouble with NuRoof!

Eventually, Jan and I got into the cab next to the truck driver and we were heading for home. What a relief! The nightmare was coming to an end and finally, I was going home to my family and would get to meet my new daughter, Dawn.

CHAPTER 28

Celebrity status!

When I arrived on camp and headed to our new flat, I wondered if I'd gone to the wrong place because the apartment was crowded with so many people wanting to see the new baby on the block. We had become a celebrity family! All I wanted though was to be alone with Dale, Margaret and the baby, and at last our friends dispersed leaving the four of us alone. Writing this now brings tears to my eyes, as I think of the relief I felt on reaching home after the terrible ordeal of being stranded in the outback, and about what might have happened to me and Jan. But now I was home, and with a baby daughter, just as I had hoped for!

The baby seemed so small to me that I was afraid to pick her up until Margaret showed me how, and helped me cradle her in my arms. In my mind's eye she smiled at me, her dad who will do whatever it takes to protect her and keep her safe for as long as he can. Dale probably wondered what all the fuss was about and soon disappeared to play with his pals.

 "Have you got a name for her, love?" I asked; believe it or not she said 'Dawn.' When I asked why 'Dawn', Margaret said it was because she was born when daylight was breaking. I think she was about to add something else when I jumped in and told her about my night in the outback and how I knew our baby girl's name was 'Dawn'. I felt this was a very romantic moment because we had both been separately inspired by the rising sun to think of the same name for our daughter.

"Silly beggar!" she said, smiling. "It's not really because she was born at dawn, it's because you can't shorten the name, can you?" I thought about how Margaret had never liked people shortening her own name. From the first moment we met she wanted me to call her 'Margaret', never 'Maggie' or 'Peg'. Our son became 'Dale' for the same reason – a name that couldn't be shortened. Ever truthful my Margaret, but the sweet romance of the moment had been a bit spoilt! At least we agreed on a name, if not the reason for it.

Over the next few weeks, we spent a lot of time together because there wasn't much work at NuRoof and I took some time off; I wasn't sure they'd want me back after the night episode with the broken-down ute. Margaret was caring for Dawn and regaining some strength before returning to work. She told me about her time in the hospital after I left her; poor lass was in labour for over twenty-four hours and needed a D&C (dilation and curettage) procedure to stop the heavy bleeding after giving birth. On top of that, she came down with flu-like symptoms for a couple of days, same as she had done after giving birth to Dale. The doctors kept her in the hospital for a few days to make sure everything was okay with both mum and baby – Dawn needed incubating for a short time after birth. Hearing all this I felt even more guilty that I'd left her on her own and I cursed myself. I hugged her until she told me to stop.

Now that I was back, I could help as much as possible and to give Margaret a break each day, I went for a walk around the camp pushing Dawn in her pram. My, did I feel proud! I stopped and chatted to whoever was around and wandered over to us. We were a bit of an attraction; since we had arrived, I didn't remember seeing anyone else on camp with a baby.

Sam and Maureen had visited Margaret when she was in the hospital and they came to see us in our flat. Sam told me that Jan had left NuRoof, I wondered where he went. Gerry and family came visiting too and their girls loved to take Dawn out in her pram and push her around the camp. Margaret was getting stronger with the help of the meals Dale and I sneaked out of the canteen – she didn't go there herself when Dawn was very small because it would have been too noisy for the baby, and she might have added to the din by crying.

Margaret was recovering for about six weeks before she said she was ready to go back to her weekend work at the hospital. It was my job to take care of Dale and Dawn when Margaret was at work, and one of my weekend highlights was pushing Dawn over to the hospital to meet her mum when she finished her shift. A lot of the staff used to come out to coo over our baby girl. She had blonde hair just like I did at her age; I kept mine until I was about seventeen when it turned dark brown, but not as dark as Margaret's near-black hair, although we don't know what colour it was when she was born. Dawn's eyes were brown just like mine, I was a proud dad alright!

CHAPTER 29

I become a stay-at-home dad, we're both fine and fined

One day after work Margaret told me that one of her workmates, Terry - a woman who called herself a Geordie and was from Hartlepool - had booked her passage back to the UK and would return by the end of the year. This news made me think it was almost time for us to book our tickets, and we planned to visit the travel agents in the next few weeks. For the time-being though, we were enjoying being a family of four, getting used to new routines and enjoying the comforts of our new flat.

Roofing work was still very slack at this time, although there were murmurings of a job coming-up in the outback. A few more of these and we would have enough money to pay our fares home, which meant I wasn't too worried about having spells of little or no local work. Instead, I was enjoying being a 'stay-at-home' dad, promenading with my daughter around camp every day and making sure Dale got off to school with his peanut butter sandwiches and flask of coffee when his mam needed a lie-in.

One day I collected our post from the camp office and found a large, official-looking brown envelope whose contents read, 'We would like to inform you that because you and your wife did not vote in the local elections you are both fined [?] dollars each.' I can't recall the exact amount, it wasn't much but it was still a shock to think we had broken some law we didn't even know about, and with all the excitement of the past few weeks we didn't even know there was an election. Thankfully, the penalty was only a small fine and not a spell in the clink!

CHAPTER 30

Happy days

This was a period when our lives felt good and we were happy, even Dale went a-wandering less often and spent more time with us. He sometimes offered to hold and feed his baby sister, although I don't suppose he told his pals that, I know I wouldn't have at his age! Occasionally, we got a surprise visitor and one day there was a knock on our door, Margaret opened it to a very tall woman called Doreen who was from the other side of the camp. She told us she had heard of the baby and would like to knit a gift for her, and invited us over to her home to take a look at all the different types of items she knitted. We took her up on this kind offer and visited her home, which was still a Nissen hut. My, what a talented lady – she could knit anything and everything: soft toys, jumpers, socks, baby clothes and scarves. To this day, I don't know why she knitted so many scarves, perhaps she gave them to the Grayland migrants who were returning back to their homelands? Perhaps the scarves helped them adapt to the cooler-than-Australia temperatures they found on returning home.

Doreen said her husband went to work up North – to the same place as Kitty's - and she hadn't heard from him since he left over six months ago! I think she must have spent most of her free time knitting and bought the wool in Perth because there's no way she could have brought all of it with her from England. We quickly became friends and Doreen joined our gang of Pommie pals.

I don't know if part of the reason for us feeling so happy was due to approaching the final stretch of our allotted two-year period in Australia. Being over here for a full two years meant there would be no penalties to pay to the Australian Government when we left. We could return to Britain with all of our hard-earned money and not forfeit anything, that was the agreement every Ten Pound Pom signed.

It was almost time to pay a visit to the travel agents and book our passage on a liner back to the UK. We would also need to visit the shipping company to find out how, and when we should pack the crates and luggage ready for transportation. Our friends from Liverpool and Bradford had lived on Graylands for more than two years and already knew their sailing dates. Oh dear, what a sad day that would be, to say 'Goodbye' to them on the quayside at Fremantle. In the meantime, I got a message through the camp's office that work had picked up at NuRoof, and would I go along to see them. This news surprised me after the carry-on Jan and I had a few weeks ago; I thought my working days with that company were probably done, but I was wrong.

I was given some local roofing work, which would suit me just fine until Margaret was back to full-strength and felt okay at the prospect of me being away for a week at a time. I was surprised when I was given the use of a new ute, I expected the bosses would buy something second-hand and cheap. The old one that let us down was well and truly burnt out, it must have had a few hundred thousand miles on the clock and was finished. Most of the time, my workmate was Bruno; he was pleased to hear the news of our baby daughter and wanted to hear all about Margaret's health, how she was getting on and what Dale thought of his new sister.

Out of nowhere he asked, "Yorkie, you return to England, yes?" This took me aback because as far as I could remember, I hadn't shared our plans with anyone. How did he know? I didn't want the bosses at NuRoof to find out in case they sacked me, and yet, this wouldn't really matter because I could get another job somewhere else, even in the outback with more money when Margaret had recovered. Then Bruno said, "I wish to return to my own country." He left it at that, and I had learnt not to ask, if he wanted to say more, he would.

CHAPTER 31

Our Kid jmps ship and pays us a visit

The time for Brian's visit had almost arrived. We decided he would stay with us in our flat and come along to the canteen with me and Dale for his meals, no-one would be any the wiser. When the big day came, I drove the new ute to meet him at Fremantle. Oh my, what an emotional greeting that was! My sister's son - who had grown-up with me like a younger brother - standing there on the quayside, both of us as far away from our homeland as it was possible to be. Uncle and nephew, brothers shedding tears of joy and hugging each other, happy to be together again.

Brian had seven days leave from the navy before he needed to return to Fremantle for transfer back to his ship, the *HMS Kent*. I lugged his large kitbag into the back of the ute.

"Brian, it looks like you're ready to hit the town, big time?"

"Course I am, I've been at sea for months!"

"Then prepare yourself, me lad, you're going to be disappointed!" On the drive back to Perth I tried to let him down gently by describing Graylands and how far out of town we were. He didn't seem too bothered though, and seemed happy to be on dry land and in the company of family. He knew about Dawn through the letters from his mother and was soon up-to-speed with our news. He couldn't tell us much about Britain because he had been away for so long. When we reached Graylands, I stopped to show him our old Nissen hut, home for almost 18 months.

"Bloody 'ell!" he said, "my bunk on the ship is better than that!"

Margaret, Dale and Dawn were outside our accommodation block playing and chatting. When they saw us arrive, Dale came running over, Margaret picked up Dawn and came trotting over making Dawn chuckle. More tears were shed with lots of hugging and ruffling of Dale's hair. We took Brian up to the flat and proudly showed him around. Big Bertha came to life and started to move, straining against her confined space making Brian laugh until he cried.

"Bloody 'ell, it's growling at us!" Brian's swearing made Dale laugh, which set Dawn off chuckling, which triggered me and Margaret, which made Brian think his joke was very funny. He continued, "The engines on my ship don't make half as much noise as this fridge! Why do you keep it?" I answered his question by opening the fridge door revealing rows of bottles of grog and soft drinks coolly waiting for us.

For now, we enjoyed a cup of tea and caught-up with family news, as much as he knew through his mother's letters. He told us about how he was transferred in a bosun's chair from the *HMS Kent* onto the smaller vessel that docked at Fremantle. He was winched up and swung out over the choppy waves, suspended by a few straps and a plank of wood that made up the chair.

"I kept my eyes tight shut until I was lowered onto the smaller ship's deck," he said, and I would have done the same too. I don't know where he'd got them from, perhaps he'd docked somewhere else during his current stint at sea, but he brought presents for Dawn - a soft toy, Dale - a toy car, and Margaret - a silk scarf. What a great feeling it was, all of us being together. More happy times!

Brian, me holding Dawn, and Margaret outside our apartment block

Margaret and Dawn weren't going along to the canteen yet for their meals, so Dale and me, we made sure we brought enough food back for them. I explained the canteen routine to Brian and gave him Margaret's knife, fork and spoon to borrow.

"Keep close to me and Dale, and don't speak to us," although I'm not sure why this seemed important! "This cutlery," I held up the knife, fork and spoon, "are the keys to a magic kingdom where you can have as many chips and as much steak as you want!" Brian's eyes lit up.

"Bloody 'ell, when can we go?" Dale laughed again at Brian's swearing, which made Dawn chuckle that spread to Margaret and me, and again, Brian thought he was a very funny man! When we got to the canteen it was full of people and there was almost no chance of Brian being singled-out by the staff as a stranger, and anyway, they were too busy serving-up the food to notice. Brian wolfed everything down and said the food was better than on his ship. He made the most of it during his visit and said he enjoyed every mouthful.

Not far from Perth was a racecourse called 'The Trots' at Gloucester Park where horses pulled traps around a big circular track. The jockeys sat inside the traps and the first horse and trap to complete three full laps was the winner. The horses were only allowed to trot round and not break into a canter. Brian wanted to go and see what it was like, so one evening Margaret, Dale, Brian and me, we decided to have a rare evening out. We left Dawn with Gerry and Lil and squeezed into the front seat of the ute. There weren't any passenger seats and it wouldn't have been much fun sitting in the open trailer at the back, so we packed ourselves into the front seats for the half-hour journey to the racecourse.

Dale in front of some of the larger carriages on show at The Trots, Gloucester Park

The grounds of the Trots were very attractive with a pleasant atmosphere. There were plenty of colourful tents selling grog; bright lights illuminated a large circular area where people were betting on the game, Two-up. I first came across the game at a job up North near Port Hedland. For such a simple game of chance, hundreds of dollars were won and lost on just a few flicks of the coins. The spinner – the man flicking the coins into the air using a paddle or 'kip' – was good, and flicked them high into the air, building a few seconds of tension for the gamblers eager to see if they had won on their two-heads or two-tails bet. We didn't bet anything, we just stood and watched. I was watching the faces of the betters as much as the coins, and was amazed by their expressions of hope turning to disappointment and sometimes joy when they won. They seemed to be in an altered state, which maybe was how some of the workers up North had lost a whole week's wages in one night.

We didn't bet on Two-up but we couldn't come to The Trots and not place a bet on the horses. Margaret, for some reason that wasn't clear, decided to place a bet on one of the outsiders called 'Whiskey Mac'. Brian and I said it had no chance and even Dale chimed in with, "Bad choice, mam." But, what do you know, on the third lap Whiskey Mac was making gains as the field of horses and traps rounded the final bend approaching the long straight.

"Come on, Whiskey Mac!!" shouted Margaret, blushing when she realised she was shouting. Brian, Dale and me, we all joined in, "Come on, Whiskey Mac, you can do it!" and he did! We cheered and jumped around as he crossed the line. Margaret's outsider came in first, and she won a fair amount of money.

"Why did you choose him, love?" I asked.

"Because, don't you remember, Brian's mum's dog is called 'Whiskey Mac.'"

Of course! I had forgotten all about him! Mind you, I didn't like him much, miserable little bugger of a Scottish terrier with a long face and a bad temper to go with it. We watched another race or two, this time without betting, before collecting Margaret's winnings and driving home. A brilliant night was enjoyed by us all.

While Brian was with us, he was treated like a celebrity by all of our friends who were keen to meet him and listen to his tales of life at sea. He lapped up the attention and thought he was the bees' knees for the week, but all too soon it was time for him to return to his ship. I didn't have the ute to take him back to Fremantle, so I asked Gerry if I could borrow his car. On the drive to the docks, we tried to be as cheery as possible but we were all feeling a bit sad, except for Dawn who was too young to know what was going on, although she perhaps picked up on the atmosphere.

The HMS Kent had reached Fremantle docks and was ready and waiting for all the Navy lads onshore to return. More tears and hugs, then Brian slung his giant kitbag over his shoulder.

"See you in a year, Our Kid!" I said.

"Cheeky bugger, you're the kid 'round here!" Dale sniggered at 'bugger', which made Dawn chuckle, which made Margaret and me laugh and once again, 'Our Kid' thought he was a very funny man!

We waved him aboard and stood watching while the large Royal Navy frigate's ramp was raised, and the ship slowly inched away from the harbour. All the navy lads were standing on the deck waving at the crowd on the quayside, who were waving back at them. On the drive back home, we stopped at a local ice-cream café to cheer ourselves up, and it helped, but we were a bit down for the next few days until our regular routines took over again.

Brian's ship, the *HMS Kent*. The red pen drawing off the bow of the ship, is Brian's attempt to draw the winch mechanism that transferred him to the smaller vessel bound for Fremantle

CHAPTER 32

We place a deposit on a big decision and a spicey meal nearly gets me killed

The time had come for us to pay a visit to the travel agent in Perth and book our passage back to the UK. We were planning to leave around October time, and managed to get four berths (including one for Dawn) on the 24,000 tonne, Italian cruise liner called the *Angelina Lauro*, leaving in late September. We would be at sea for three weeks, calling at Cape town, South Africa and Tenerife. Dale and I were excited by the thought of being at sea, but poor Margaret was dreading it. She had never liked travelling across water and even when we had been out in a rowing boat on the lakes in the parks in Hull, had got off the boat feeling wobbly and a bit sick. We didn't have a choice to return to Britain any other way, the airfares at that time were far too costly. The fares home on the liner came to 1,999 Australian dollars, the equivalent of nearly £9,000 in today's (2023) money. We only needed to leave a deposit at the time of booking. The airfares would have cost even more and the journey completed in several stages. I hoped that Margaret would adapt to life at sea – three weeks would be long enough to find out!

I breathed a big sigh of relief when we paid our deposits, the decision was well and truly made, we were returning home. All we needed to do between now and our leaving date, was to earn enough money to pay the balance of our fares. This meant I would need to work in the outback to do a few jobs there, and I thought of Sam, he was sure to have one or two jobs lined-up for us.

Margaret realised that we had booked our berths on the same liner as her workmate, Terry. On one of our weekend strolls to meet Dawn's mam from work, Terry came over to see us and started talking about how we would all be on the same liner back home. I said I thought it would be a good idea if we all stuck together during the voyage and she agreed. I hoped that Terry would keep Margaret company during the trip and that might help her to feel less sick. That was the hope.

The noticeboard at Graylands soon came up trumps with an advert: 'Aluminium Roofing Workers Wanted for work up North, Transport

Arranged, Good Pay and Accommodation included.' *Great, I thought, this would be easy, done all this before and it's money towards our fare home.* After talking it over with Margaret I signed-up and a week later was on my travels again. Kitbag in-hand, including my own toolkit with my top tool – the trusty blue hammer, I was picked up at Perth railway station in the biggest ute I had ever seen. It needed to be big to accommodate the six or more workers squeezed into the temporary seating at the back. We drove about 300 miles (480 kilometres) north into the outback to a worksite where a lot of lightly constructed buildings were being erected.

The temperature was falling as we headed into autumn, but the humidity was increasing, and the days were becoming very muggy, which wasn't much of a relief from the heat of summer. There were many, many different nationalities of workers on site and it was noticeable that none of them were Australian except for the few bosses watching their crews here and there. Our site accommodation was Nissen huts, long ones that could take twelve bunks, six down each side. On the whole site there was a single toilet in a tin hut, and it wasn't a place you wanted to be for very long at a time, if at all. Many of us, and me included (most of the time) took ourselves over to the scrubland instead.

Every night the drinking and gambling on Two-up began and finished when some of the gamblers ran out of money. The grog was brought in on the weekly visit from the stores wagon, along with the food the on-site canteen cooked-up for us. I realised that these conditions and this lifestyle was the future for some of these workers; those who spent their dollars boozing and gambling, they would never save up enough money to get back to their home countries. Maybe they weren't really bothered even though they said they wanted to go back. Maybe drinking and gambling was the only way they could cope with life out here. I was lucky, I had my family to think about and focus on, I was doing this work for all of us and we were going back home – and soon.

I brought with me a small battery-powered radio and spent my evenings trying to get it to tune into a station, but with no luck. Perhaps we were too far away from any radio transmitters. When the radio didn't work, I wrote letters to Margaret and Dale describing my day's work and what I had seen that day. The letters travelled back to Perth on the light aircraft that dropped off other weekly supplies the wagon couldn't fetch, plus a few workers coming onto site and took a few others back to Perth. This time I had a couple of workmates, both of them Polish and we made a good team. By now, I felt like an old hand at this game and was no longer green like I was that first time working with Sam.

We got into the habit of going for a quick break to get something to eat around eleven in the morning, then continued until about three in the afternoon when we finished for the day. We bought the food from the shop part of the canteen, probably some of it was left-over food from the previous day that had been re-heated. One day I ate something with a bit more spice in it than I was used to, then went back to work. A few hours later I needed to go to the loo – fast! I climbed down from the roof as quick as I could and ran over to the tin hut. I slammed through the door and lifted the toilet lid.

"Jesus H. Christ!" I shouted. A stinging hellhole met my eyes; small redback spiders everywhere, covering the lid, crawling out of the toilet pan and heading towards my legs. I turned and ran shouting, "Redbacks! Redbacks!" and disappeared into the scrub to relieve myself.

Another lucky escape, a bite from a couple of those little buggers and I could have been a goner, they're one of the most venomous spiders in Australia. By the time I was walking back from the scrub, a couple of workers were on their way over to the tin hut and within minutes it was in flames. When eventually the fire died down, I went over to investigate and whatever they had used had burned hot because the metal had begun to twist. I didn't go back and use it as a toilet though, the scrub became my permanent place from then on. Back on the roof I told my workmates what happened, and they said they heard that someone was bitten.

One time after we had finished for the day, I was feeling a bit bored and decided to go for a stroll into the scrub towards a water tank I had spotted from the roof top. It was near one of the worksite's open-air toilets. I thought I would combine spending a penny with an exploration, because I hadn't seen a water tank so close to a worksite before and wanted to investigate. I told my two workmates where I was going, took my trusty hammer and wore my protective goggles, because you had to be prepared out there.

The water tank was a large steel cylinder about 30 feet tall, 20 feet across, (nine by six metres) quite rusty looking on the outside, and a ladder ran vertically from its bottom to the top. These tanks used to supply the local population in the days before pipes were laid to carry water from the dams and reservoirs. I knew before I reached the top of the ladder that this one was no longer used, the stench wafting over the top was terrible and along with it came swarms of flies. They flew straight towards me but my goggles meant I could still see through the thick black cloud of them into the tank below. I don't know if something had fallen and died in there, the smell was horrendous. The water level was low and the surface was covered in thick green algae.

There was nothing else to see in there so I started to climb back down and there, close to the bottom of the ladder was a joey kangaroo staring up at me. What a lovely looking animal with large brown eyes, standing about two and a half to three feet (about one metre) tall. Maybe he was thinking I was lovely looking too because he just kept staring at me, fixed to the spot. I didn't know what to do and slowly got down from the ladder back onto solid ground, that's when I heard a loud thumping sound. The little joey's parents appeared from around the tank stamping their back feet on the earth kicking up some dust. They were massive, at least seven feet (just over two metres) tall and didn't look too happy with me. Believe it or not, they raised their paws ready to box to protect their joey.

Suddenly, I was engulfed by fear and knew I shouldn't run. Instinctively, I took the hammer and began to hit the side of the water tank.

"BoooOOooM! BoooOOooM!" reverberated the tank.

By this point, the biggest kangaroo was really eyeballing me, so I banged the tank harder and faster and the noise echoed and amplified as it bounced around inside the nearly empty tank. Eventually, the parents dropped their clenched boxing fists, turned and all three of them hopped away, so fast that in seconds they were out-of-sight. By now my heart was pounding away in my chest, and I slumped to the ground, suddenly drained of energy. From somewhere behind me I heard voices.

"Yorkie! You ok?" It was my workmates come to find me. They said they knew I had gone 'into the scrub for business,' when they heard the banging, they decided to check everything was ok. I told them what happened.

"Yorkie, you are very lucky man!"

"Saved by my hammer!" I replied, waving it in front of me. "I'll be back in a few minutes, lads" I said to my workmates, "I still have some business to attend to!" The open-air toilet facility was round the other side of the tank, and was where all the flies came from, but I'd take flies and kangaroos any day over redbacks.

A few days later, there was excitement of a different kind when out-of-the-blue there was lots of shouting and the sound of vehicles' engines starting-up. Our gang was told to get down from the roof, climb in the ute and 'get lost' for a while. As we drove away, a couple of trucks were approaching the worksite that by now was like a ghost town, not a single worker was left on site. From the in-coming trucks came the blaring of, 'Union! Union!' We carried on driving towards the nearest town - more like a village really and hung out there for a few hours until we were told to pile back in the ute and return to the worksite.

We found out later that the construction workers' unions were trying to recruit members, but nobody wanted anything to do with them. What must they have thought when they reached a building site with no-one on it? I heard that this area was a favourite spot of the non-union employers. I didn't mind, I remember how I felt about unions before we left the UK. In my opinion, they were getting out of hand what with calling for workers to 'down tools' and go on strike all the time. They were nearly bringing the UK to a standstill, and the same would happen over here if they got their way.

When grown-up Dawn read the previous paragraph, she told me that I had an upside-down view of the unions, and how it didn't make any sense for me to be complaining about the conditions we were working under, and then paint the unions as the villains. They were the ones trying to get construction workers like me better working conditions, better pay and protection. I told her that she hadn't lived through the 1960s in Britain, and of course she couldn't answer that! In the end, we had to agree to disagree on the matter, except I've included this because there's the

145

chance that she was right, that if we had joined the union back then the working conditions might have improved. In reality though, I think the bosses would have paid us less wages to cover the higher costs of providing better working conditions. Who knows! It's all water under the bridge now.

CHAPTER 33

We find a mystery noise unsettling

I worked at this site for about a month before returning to Graylands; during that time, I hadn't shaved at all and returned home with a big bushy beard. When I walked through the door of our flat, Dawn was crawling about on the mat, she looked up at me and I bent down to pick her up.

"Whah! Whah!" she cried, turning round and crawling away as fast as her chubby little arms and legs would take her. She made for the table and hid under there until Margaret bent down and scooped her up.

Me with a ('Teddy Boy') bouffant, bursting with pride, holding Dawn

"Don't be silly," she said softly, "it's your dad, he's just got a big beard that's all. Very soon, he's going to shave it off, aren't you, love?" I took the hint and headed for the bathroom. By the time I came out, beardless, Dale was home.

"Hello son, what are you doing home so early?" He told me that a few of his friends had gone, their families had left the camp for other states in Eastern Australia. Margaret told me later that Dale had spent more time at home during the month I was away and was taking more interest in his sister, helping out and even feeding her. He made sure she was covered-up when they went out for walks with the pram and pulled the hood across the top of the pram to prevent the magpies from pecking her head. Dale had found out the name of the birds that couldn't resist flying down to peck his head!

Sam and family paid us a visit and we all went on another trip to Cottlesloe Beach. I had recently told Sam that we were booked on a liner to return to the UK and since then, his attitude towards me changed. I was sure of it, although Margaret didn't seem to notice. I think he felt let down and maybe a bit hurt that we were leaving. As I've already mentioned, Sam saw me as a younger brother and our two families got on well. His real younger brother died and left him, and now I was leaving him by choosing life in England over the life he had helped me build over here. Perhaps he felt rejected. Margaret and I knew that Maureen wanted to go back to England, which was another reason for Sam to distance himself - he knew she would want to follow us.

Most of the money I earnt from the recent work away, went towards paying for our crates and boxes of worldly goods that had already travelled half-way around the globe, to travel the other half with us back to England later in the year. The reality that we were going home was sinking in, and although I was certain it was the right decision for my family, I had a few occasions when I had small doubts. These usually happened when we had our regular get-togethers with friends on camp; when we spotted new immigrants - who were easy to identify because they looked very pale and lost - we invited them along too. From our own experience, we knew this would help settle them in, and we could pass on our own life-tips learnt from hard experience.

In those days, there was nothing in-place to welcome new arrivals, no counselling to help them settle in. We got off the plane, were transferred to the camp and that was it, left to get on with it and make our own way. For many of us, it was the first time we had ever left our own country, and we went from hometowns where we grew-up to another continent on the other side of the world in a matter of days. When I look back, I can understand why a lot of us returned to our home countries.

We were enjoying living in our new flat until one night, there was a loud booming noise coming from somewhere in the apartment. Once it began it returned every night, and sometimes was so loud it either woke us up or we couldn't get to sleep. At first, we thought it was Big Bertha 'singing' a new tune, but then we realised it began at about the same time every night and that didn't match Big Bertha at all. After a bit more investigation inside the flat and finding nothing to cause the racket, we traced the source to the outside drain that our bathroom pipes ran in to. Perhaps there was an animal inside the drain making the noise.

One evening as dusk was falling, I took my trusty blue hammer and banged like mad on the ground by the drain, thinking that whatever was down there would have one hell of a headache by sunrise. How wrong can you be? Over the next few nights, the booming got louder and lasted longer, none of us could sleep, except Dawn who seemed oblivious to it. We couldn't put up with it any longer, I reported it to the office and was told someone would come along shortly to take a look.

Margaret was at work the weekend two Australian (yes, Australian!) workmen turned up to investigate. Dale and I were keen to find out what was making the booming sound and we tagged along to find out what the workmen were doing. What was lurking in the drains? Some sort of giant frog we wondered? The workmen soon had the drain covers off, and fed a tube with a light at one end down into the darkness. They let Dale and me take a look but all we could see was blackness.

"Have you seen more of the large ants lately, mate?" asked one of the workmen. We had noticed that in the last month there were more black ants than usual, and they were larger than the regular ants we were used to seeing around the place. With that, the workmen nodded at one another.

"We know what's causing the noise, mate, and we'll have it fixed for you in a jiffy." They explained that at night, large ants make their way down the drains to find moist earth, and these large ants provide a very tasty meal for bullfrogs. Either this massive bullfrog followed the ants into the drain one night and realised he was onto a good thing – every night dinner would come to him, or he hopped into the drain one night when out exploring and stayed there for the same reason – a good meal on his doorstep. Every night, he went a-croaking to attract a lady frog, and having a belly full of large, black ants he had enough energy to bellow all night, until one lucky lady frog crossed his path. His bellowing bounced around the drain and up the pipe leading to our bathroom, amplified along its way.

The workmen spread some dry chemicals all around the base of the apartment block and sealed the drains. Then they pumped some liquid chemicals down into the drains and said they would be back in a week's time to check on the situation and remove the drain seals. Knowing there was a massive bullfrog living in our drains put a dampener on our feelings about the flat, how often could we expect this to happen?

For the next few nights, the noise was horrendous, the croaking got even louder and seemed to have changed somehow. We got next-to-no sleep until the booming stopped. I don't know what the liquid pumped into the drains did, but it was horrible to think the frog was being poisoned and dying slowly, or maybe he was shouting for food, or complaining because his ideal home set-up had been ruined and he couldn't escape.

By the end of that week the Aussie workmen were back as promised, and they showed us some photos of bullfrogs. What a size they were, as big as my out-stretched hand! Once again, they fed the lighted telescope tube into the drain and let Dale and me take a look. All we could see was a big black lump, like a clod of earth stuck in the drainpipe. So, now we knew why the croaking changed tune and eventually stopped, the bullfrog was slowly poisoned. For a brief moment I felt sorry for the bugger, he was only trying to make his way in life and happened to choose the wrong place to make his home.

I pictured me and my family stepping onto the homeward-bound liner and smiled because I wasn't making the same mistake as the poor old bullfrog here, I was getting us out of here before it was too late. Maybe the sun *was* getting to me after all! The workmen went on to say that sometimes they needed to dig down into the drains a few feet to get to the frogs, but not this time, and they were confident the problem wouldn't return any time soon, at least not until the next mating season.

The whole experience had unnerved me and Margaret, and our new home lost its shine. At least the large ants had disappeared thanks to the chemicals the workmen put down, but we wondered what might come along next to bother us. Word had got around the camp about our bullfrog experience and our friends ribbed (or ribbit-ed!) us a bit and we laughed with them.

The make-up of the residents on camp was changing as more of our long-term friends left, including a family from Manchester and our good friends Gerry, Lil and family who returned to Liverpool. We couldn't make ourselves go and see them off at Fremantle, it was too much, too many feelings – too sad about them leaving and too worried about us leaving and wondering if it really was the right thing to be going back. I knew it was, but at the same time we'd made a life over here and maybe it was going to get better and better? Sometimes, it was all too much to think about.

CHAPTER 34

I purchase a souvenir

It was time for me to find some work again, and the same firm I'd just worked for came up trumps again with a week's work in the outback. Three of us from the last roofing job were given the work. This time we had accommodation in a hotel, and the job was in a small town, I forget the name remembering only that the town was close to an Aborigine settlement or village. The three of us worked well together and finished the roof in four days, giving ourselves some free time to go exploring. Our destination was the Aborigine village where the hotel manager told us we would be welcomed, especially if we bought some of the craft they made to sell to tourists.

We parked-up outside the village and made our way on foot towards the circle of very large boulders. Inside the circle were groups of Aboriginal people working away at their crafts – cutting and carving pieces of wood and stones. The air was filled with the sounds of chipping and carving and chattering, overlaid with occasional shouts and laughter. The boulders were covered in paintings, drawn in red, maybe animal blood or perhaps red paint? For the tourists it was 'animal blood' and the pictures told stories of hunting expeditions.

Three men were hanging around near a couple of boulders that looked like they formed the entrance to the circle and we approached them. We knew instinctively that we shouldn't step inside the circle and kept our distance to show some respect for this protected place. The men were friendly and spoke quickly and sharply, describing how they travel to the local towns to sell their craft pieces. They told us how they could find water in the driest parts of the land and how they hunted for animals. It was obvious they were proud of their heritage, but worried about the younger generations. They pointed to groups of young lads lying about and drinking. The shouts and laughter we heard earlier came from them. The three older blokes went on to tell us the younger ones didn't want to follow in their footsteps, they didn't want to hunt, they had no future.

By now, I was feeling a bit depressed and wanted to get away. I also wanted to take away a memento and asked if I could see some of their craft pieces. One of the chaps showed me a boomerang.

"50 cents" he said, adding, "this is real blood from hunting," pointing to red, drying stains covering the outer curved edge. I wasn't too happy about the blood but liked the idea of taking home a boomerang, and out came my 50 cents (equivalent to about £4 in 2023). We thanked the chaps and walked away back to the ute. I felt some kinship with them and their way of life. As far as I had been told, my dad's family were tinkers in Ireland, travelling from town-to-town by horse and wagon, (called a 'vardo') living on the road and earning their money by repairing small household items. That sort of life didn't seem a million miles away from the life of the inhabitants of the Aborigine village. Both were hard ways to make ends meet, and the Irish tinker life might have been passed down to me, if my dad hadn't left Ireland to make a better life for himself and therefore his descendants.

The following day, we decided to return home and on our way called in at the roofing firm's small office just outside Perth. They paid us for four days work, cash-in-hand and the pay was good. I told them if anything else cropped-up to let me know. I parked the ute in the work's yard and caught a bus into Perth centre, then from there a train to Graylands. Margaret and Dale were surprised and pleased to see me back a few days early, I was keen to show her the boomerang.

 "Look what I got this time, love" I said, pleased with my purchase and waving the bloodied piece of carved wood in front of her.

"What's that on it? Let me wipe it off," she picked up a cloth and held her hand out for the boomerang.

"Quick, son let's go outside and try it out!" The two of us scarpered before Margaret could clean away part of the boomerang's history. I assumed it would be coming back with us to England but it was one of my few treasures that got away.

On Margaret's next weekend off, the four of us took the train into Perth and a bus out to Fremantle to pay the remaining balance on the cost of shipping our boxes and crates back to England. We also called in at the liner company (Lauro Lines) in Perth to find out when they wanted the remaining balance of our fare. They told us they would be in touch a month before our sailing date of 30th September. We still had most of it to pay but we weren't worried because we had been saving for months, sending some of the money back to a building Society in England and saving some of it in an Australian bank.

Dale's fare was half the adult fare and I don't know how they worked out Dawn's, but it was about one fifth of Dale's which made it about one tenth of an adult fare! Our baby Dawn was one tenth an adult, and even at that, her fare cost the equivalent of about £300 today (2023). We knew we would have enough cash to pay the balance, as long as I could keep getting work in the outback, and that hadn't been a problem yet. We had arrived in Australia with about £40 (the equivalent of about £500 nowadays – 2023) and could afford to pay our fares home (almost £1000) that were 25 times that original amount. This must have meant the wages we earnt between us were decent.

It's true we lived modestly, and we never did any single thing that cost us a lot of money, but even so, our wages were nowhere near enough to afford a mortgage, even for a small plot of land. No wonder so many immigrants on Grayland travelled eastwards in search of a permanent home; plots of land and houses in many of the towns and bigger cities were cheaper out that way. This direction wasn't for my family, we were heading further west in a few months, and every day the dream of returning home grew a step closer.

Following the bullfrog episode came a stomach-churning stench once again from the drains. A few days after reporting it at the camp office, the Aussie workmen appeared and told us the cause was the rotting carcase of the frog. They pumped down some more liquid, sealed the drains again and sprayed around the outside of the apartment block, saying they would return in a week to remove the drain seals. Eventually, the terrible stench faded, and life was back to normal in our flat.

CHAPTER 35

Changes are afoot

We continued to regularly receive letters from Elsie and when she knew we were returning home to Hull by the end of October, she offered to put us up for a few months until we found our own house. She sent us lots of newspaper clippings that showed how Hull was changing. The streets of the small two-up, two-down houses we'd grown up and lived in, were being pulled down to make way for a big new road. The families living in those houses were relocated to new properties that were shooting up across the city and on its outskirts. If we had stayed, we would be living in our own new house by now, but on the flip side we wouldn't be having this adventure of a lifetime. That's what life is sometimes - pluses and minuses!

I needed to find a job again and thought Sam might have come along with something, but we seemed to see less and less of him and Maureen and the girls. I heard he had another roofer working with him from another state. I felt a bit sad about him growing distant since I told him we were leaving, but I also knew it was hard for him. Even without Sam on the scene, it didn't take me long to find a job as a brickie's labourer on a site on the outskirts of Perth where bungalows were under construction. I travelled there on the usual steam train and started to buy the local newspaper to read on the journey home. The work was tough but that didn't bother me at all, the time passed very quickly.

One day at the building site I saw a few familiar faces – it was Bruno and a few others, workers from NuRoof doing a felting job. It was great to see a friendly face again. Bruno and I caught-up with news, chatting about a few of the NuRoof workers we both knew as well as our own family news. He said Sam had called in at the yard a few days ago and said he would be moving his family out of Western Australia by the end of the year, heading eastwards.

Richard didn't work with NuRoof any longer, he hadn't been well for a long time and his family had decided to return to Poland. Bruno also said that NuRoof wasn't getting the work like it used to, in fact it seemed to be drying up. Since hearing that, I noticed a lot of roofing-firms advertising in the paper. NuRoof was now competing with new firms just starting up. I wondered how many of them were owned by workers who had previously worked for NuRoof thinking they could strike out on their own. *Good luck to 'em!* I thought.

I thought Bruno looked much older than when we had worked together. Older and weary. He asked me if I carried a photo of my baby daughter.

"Fair dinkum I do!" I said, showing it to him.

"She a little peach!" he said, smiling and continued, "Yorkie, wherever you go, make sure you look after family!" He looked more than weary now, sad even. I told him we were leaving Australia in September.

"I wish it is my family going home to Poland!" I knew these would be the last words I would hear from Bruno. We shook hands and I thought I felt a small tremor. Had good old Bruno taken to drinking grog? He had changed, but then we all had. Working with him had been a pleasure, he was a real gent and he had helped me get through some hard times on the job. I think nowadays he would be called a great 'mentor'. Thanks Bruno!

More changes were afoot: back at Graylands the canteen food had become more varied than the regular steak and chips. They were now serving-up a wide range of tasty dishes. Maybe my tastebuds were a bit more adventurous too, especially after tasting crayfish I was keener to try new food. Another change was the size of the families arriving on camp, there were more kids than we remember seeing before. Maybe that was because some of the flats in the new apartment blocks could house larger families, whereas when it was Nissen huts, squeezing a family of four in there was too much, three was just about manageable.

Although most families didn't stay on Graylands very long (soon travelling eastwards where the land was supposed to be greener and less parched), we still had a few long-term friends on camp - Kitty and family, and Doreen-The-Knitter. This meant we weren't short of company and still had a few get-togethers, inviting some of the newbies along too. Also, thanks to Doreen, Dawn had a plentiful supply of lovely, newly knitted garments.

Around this time, we began to get regular visits from the camp manager and another official asking us if we had found alternative housing yet. Of course, these visits were unsettling, but we felt safe in the knowledge that by the time the two years were up, we would be on the liner sailing across the Indian Ocean on our way home. We did not dare tell them we were leaving Australia in case they wanted us off the camp straightaway, so instead kept telling them we were looking for housing. They believed us and after a few visits left us to get on with our lives.

CHAPTER 36

My final job in the outback has an explosive finale

I was ready for a change from the brickie's labouring job and was also tired of travelling to and from Perth by train. For some reason I kept my rail tickets for what turned out to be my final return commute to the building site, and they are framed and sitting on a shelf in my hobby room, another beloved memento from our Australian adventure. I wanted a change but suddenly, work was getting harder to find, the only jobs advertised were for skilled machine workers of all grades to work in the opencast mines up near Port Hedland for a month at a time. This meant good wages and after talking it over with Margaret, I paid a visit to the mining company's headquarters in Perth. They gave me a job with a good rate of pay and told me to be ready to fly up there in a week's time. I was nervous about leaving my family for a month and working so far away, but I knew this would be the last outback job I would ever take.

One week later I was at Perth airport with my rucksack and a small holdall, waiting along with six other blokes to board the light aircraft to take us up to the worksite near Port Hedland. I got seated and found myself next to another Pom, this time from Lincolnshire, whose real name I didn't know, instead calling him 'Whybee' as in 'Yb' for 'Yellowbelly' and of course as soon as I opened my mouth, he knew I was from Yorkshire and called me 'Yorkie'. I didn't know why people from Lincolnshire were called Yellowbellies; Yb told me the nickname originated from the yellow stain on farm workers' aprons that came from picking the mustard grown in the Lincolnshire fields.

I glanced out of the window as the plane was preparing for take-off and spotted a 747 landing – perhaps another flock of hopeful immigrants ready to embark on an uncertain future? Yb and I started chatting, I told him about my family and how we would soon be heading across the Indian Ocean back to England. Yb said he was a construction worker and brought his family over from Eastern Australia - Sydney way, to the western states. They made their way westwards by driving over 1000 miles (1600 kilometres) along the Eyre Highway across the Nullarbor Plain – over 1000 miles of flatness with nary a tree in sight, across a terrain of dry shrubland.

Arriving in Perth they rented a rundown house in the suburbs and decided that if, after another year (their fourth) in Australia they were no closer to being able to afford to buy their own property, they would return to Old Blighty. Yb was used to working in the outback around Sydney and some of the larger eastern cities. I thought we would work well together and was glad we were both headed for the same place. I told him about Margaret, Dale and Dawn back on Graylands, and we showed each other the family photos we carried in our wallets.

Mid-flight we were told the aircraft would land at Marble Bar to drop off the mail and some supplies. On landing, Yb and I climbed out of the plane to stretch our legs. Marble Bar was a small town in the desert that grew from goldmining. It's a rocky place and its name comes from a nearby outcrop (or bar) of the mineral jasper that was mistaken for marble. In between the reddish rocks the ground was sparse shrubland with bushes dotted around on the red dusty earth. We might have been on Mars ('Mars Bar' perhaps!). It was a hellhole to be sure. I was used to the outback by now, but this was a whole new level, the temperature during the day was usually over 100°F (38°C). We were in the hottest town in Australia, and we had come here to work in the mines. We'd been told we were replacing a couple of workers who were ready to return to Perth. No wonder the wages were good, no-one in their right minds would come here for anything but good money. Yb was shocked.

"What the hell have we come to, Yorkie?" I looked around at the rows of tin-roofed houses, a few Aboriginal men were sprawled around here and there. I didn't tell him our camp and working conditions up near Port Hedland wouldn't be much better.

"We're here to work, WhyBee, and we'll soon be back home with our families!" The truth though, I felt as desperate as he did and wanted to catch the next flight back to Perth, but of course that wouldn't pay our precious fares for the voyage back to Blighty. We got back on the plane for the final leg of the journey to Port Hedland, passing through some turbulence on the way that joggled us around, I didn't mind this distraction – it stopped me thinking about working in the opencast mine under the blazing sun.

The mine was the biggest worksite I'd ever worked on and full of huge, heavy machinery. The mine was opencast and above ground, which meant as much iron ore as possible was dug out before the operation moved to another site to start the process again. There were more safety regulations in-place than I'd ever seen before; the site had its own basic medical hut, and there was even a purpose-built shower block, but the sleeping accommodation was still very basic – rows of bunk beds in a big room.

Me and Yb, we stuck together and our job was to keep the iron ore flowing along a conveyor belt. A massive machine dug deeper and deeper into the solid earth loosening a mixture of iron ore, rock and of course loads of dust. Excavators with bucket arms then scooped up this mix and deposited it into very large dumper trucks. The trucks drove round to the conveyor belt and slowly tipped their load onto it. Yb and me, we had to rake off everything making sure only the iron ore reached the top of the belt, and from there it fell into the back of the lorries. The lorries took it to Port Hedland from where some of it was loaded onto railway goods wagons and then taken to other parts of Australia, and the rest of it loaded onto ships and taken to other parts of the world.

At that time, exporting iron ore to the rest of the world from Australia was just taking-off; over the years the market grew, and iron ore is now one of Australia's biggest exports. I think they must now have a more sophisticated system than two blokes with rakes, although maybe it's 2000 blokes with rakes! It was back-breaking work and in those conditions of sweltering heat, thick red dust that at times got so thick it blocked out the sun, and clamouring noise, I thought I'd committed a crime I'd forgotten about (perhaps smuggling out the soft toys from the low security prison?) and I'd been sent to Hell as a punishment.

One really good thing this worksite had going for it was the canteen – the meals were very tasty and looking forward to them helped to keep up our morale. We needed something to get us through some unpleasant experiences that happened every day, like being covered in flies. As I said, the work was really hard and made us drip with sweat constantly. At certain times of the day swarms of flies appeared, landed on areas of uncovered skin and stuck there attracted to the sweat, maybe for a drink!

We soon learnt when the swarms were about to appear and made sure we put our tops back on before they arrived. Nevertheless, they found our bare skin wherever it was exposed, and there was nothing else to do but put up with the blighters.

There were loads of us workers, many more than I had ever seen before. We were split into gangs and each gang had a ganger and groups of gangers were told what to do by site foremen. The work went on all day and often through the night with lorries coming and going transporting their loads to Port Hedland. On about the fourth day, the ganger of our team came strolling over to me.

"Hey mate, you're a Pom, right?" I nodded. "Ever taken charge of a digger or dumper?" I nodded again. "Think you can handle one of these beauts?" he asked, pointing at a massive dumper truck. It was about four times the size of anything I had worked on in Hull and to be honest, the thought of manoeuvring that monster around the site was daunting. But I knew that being inside the cabin was a chance to get a bit of shelter from the blazing sun, and some protection from the flies, and I nodded again. I was surprised at how easy the truck was to handle and found myself driving around the site within no time, dumping the mix of earth, ore and dust onto the conveyor belt for some other workers to rake through.

When the sun went down and most of the workers downed tools and had eaten in the canteen, the gambling started on the familiar Two-up game. Following that, came the fighting between workers belonging to different gangs and between winners and losers of Two-up. They made an almighty rumpus and probably ended up in the medical hut by the end of the night. Yb and me, we kept our distance from them and after chatting for a bit were usually so knackered after the day's work, we soon dropped off to sleep, ready to begin again the following day.

By the end of that first week, I was taken off the dumper truck because it was needed at another site. My next job was to be a powder monkey working with dynamite explosives. Where the earth and rock were so hard the digger couldn't make headway, I had to drill some holes into it with a massive hand drill, pack the holes with dynamite, fix fuse wire to the dynamite, light the fuse then run like the clappers. The site's safety regulations were a bit slack in this area because all I was supposed to do

161

was sound a horn to warn the nearby workers. Luckily, even though there were always loads of them milling about, no-one got hurt during the time I was there.

Yb was stuck raking ore off the conveyor belt and one evening started to talk about the workers arriving and leaving on the light airplane. I could tell he had had enough and was thinking of getting a ride to Port Hedland. By morning he was packed and ready to go, telling me that this job was a step too far into Hell for him.

We shook hands and his last words to me were, "Give my regards to Old Blighty, and Yorkie, look after that family of yours!" I was sorry to see him go but understood his reasons; I reckoned I could work about another fortnight then I'd be on a light aircraft myself back to Port Hedland and from there back home to Perth.

For the next week I wasn't put to work on the conveyor belt again, instead, I was put back on the dumper when it returned to our site. There was a dumper driver whose face I thought I recognised but couldn't think where from. During one of our regular water-breaks I found out where, when he came over to me.

"Are you Yorkie from NuRoof?" I nodded. "We worked together on a job down near Albany." *Christ,* I thought, *I am in Hell*! This was the bloke who creeped me out. I swear he was the twin of the bloke in the stamp and coins shop in London Court in Perth. I didn't trust either one of them, they both gave me the creeps. If he did tell me his name, I've long forgotten it. 'Twin Man' is how I think of him now.

Another ten days or say wore on and I was well into my third week when I began to feel a bit 'off.' I didn't think I'd make it through another week and wanted to get on the next light aircraft leaving for Perth. The problem was, I didn't have the money to pay my fare back. If you worked for the time you signed-up for - a month in my case - you got a free return flight, but if you left early, you had to pay the fare home. I never carried more than I needed in the outback, and that wasn't enough to buy a flight back because I expected to do my time when I signed-up.

Twin Man and I got talking and I told him I wanted to leave, he said he was flying back in a couple of days and would lend me the fare to fly home too.

I couldn't believe it, *this* coming from *him* wrong-footed me. Were my feelings about him wrong? Why would he do that? Anyway, I was fading fast physically and mentally and agreed, thinking I could pay him back a few days after we got home and I'd been to the bank. A part of me wondered if he was playing a trick, making me think I was going home only to be told at the last minute to get off the plane because I didn't have the fare. But no, he was true to his word, when the day came, there we both were on the light aircraft bound for Perth.

At Port Hedland a lady boarded and took the seat next to me and we started chatting. She was a Cockney - also a £10 Pom - living in Port Hedland for quite a few years by now. She and her husband were another pair of Poms that had failed to get on the housing ladder and had finally decided to pack-in and return to the UK. Her husband was still working at Port Hedland and would be flying back to Britain in a few weeks, and she was returning in a few days. I told her that my family were going back home in a few months. We talked about the countryside back home and she welled-up describing the lush, green fields of Kent where she used to go hop-picking as a girl. Baby butterflies in my belly began fluttering at the thought of being back in Yorkshire, and my uneasiness at owing a debt to Twin Man was forgotten for a few minutes.

On landing at Perth, Twin Man said he would call a taxi and take me to meet his family. All I wanted to do was go home but he had lent me the airfare back so I felt I had to go along. He kept saying, "It's ok, don't worry, pay me back when you get back to Graylands." But somehow, there was nothing this man could say that would put me at my ease, and yet he'd lent me the fare. It was a very confusing state to be in.

Eventually, we arrived at his place and I was completely shocked; the house was a run-down shack and should have been demolished years ago, and the smell coming from it was horrendous. Although there were other people in the house, no-one came out to welcome him home. When we got through the front door, he started talking loudly in a European language that I didn't recognise. That's when fear began to creep over me because I had no clue what he was saying. I asked him about getting a lift back to Graylands and he smiled, weirdly.

"Have a meal with us, Yorkie. One of my family drive you to camp later." Out came the grog and the whole family became lively, they started talking to each other, laughing and making strange noises.

Six or seven of us sat down around a makeshift table to eat the meal. I don't remember who cooked it, but Twin Man called it 'Hungarian Goulash' so maybe they were all Hungarian. I managed a couple of spoonfuls – not spoons like I was used to, these were more like chopsticks – when I realised I needed the toilet and I needed it fast! Of course, this brought lots of laughs and pats on the backs. I was shown to the toilet 'shed', it had no running water and was more of a box containing a small amount of water plonked on the ground in an outhouse tacked on to the side of the shack. There were rags to clean yourself instead of toilet paper. I promised myself I would never eat goulash again and to this day I've never been good with spices.

All of a sudden, a stick of dynamite came rolling through the gap under the toilet door. Luckily, by this time I had finished and cleaned myself. Panic-stricken by the sight of the dynamite I burst out of the toilet, grabbed my holdall and made a quick exit as fast as I could, leaving behind the sound of raucous laughter and shouting from those sun-baked, crazy fools.

Thinking back, the 'dynamite' must have been some kind of flare they kept around the place, because the dynamite on site at the mine works was kept under strict control. I soon hitched a lift back to Graylands and expected Twin Man to appear any day for the money he paid out for me, but he never did. There was no way I was going back to his place to give him the money. From the minute I met him I knew he was a wrong-un, and I figured I'd paid back my dues with the entertainment he and his family got when they fed me goulash.

CHAPTER 37

The final few months

The following couple of months passed by in a blur, I got some more local work with NuRoof, Margaret continued with her regular shifts at the hospital, and Dale went back and forth to school and spent more time with us and less time going off on his own adventures. He told me about an occasion when he and his pals were wandering around the camp; they were over by the canteen watching a ute making a delivery, when a cloud of loud, buzzing insects appeared. Within a minute, the back of the ute was completely covered in bees.

Dale and his mates watched from behind a wall, transfixed by the sight as the driver came back out of the canteen with empty-looking containers. He took one look at the bee-covered bed of his ute, dropped the containers and ran towards the camp office. A few of the bees left the ute for the containers, perhaps they had contained sugar or syrup, something sweet that attracted them. Maybe some of it had spilled over the back of the ute.

Dale and his mates were still watching when minutes later the camp's manager appeared, and shortly after that a couple of men in another ute, this one carrying some equipment to draw the bees away from the delivery ute. The blokes put on their protective gear, puffed some smoke from a pair of bellows over the bees and somehow coaxed them into a box; job done, they drove away with the boxed and sleepy bees. The delivery man threw his containers into the back of his now bee-free ute and drove away. The excitement and buzz over, the lads went off somewhere else on the camp to see what they could find.

Dawn was growing day-by-day and was using the furniture and whatever she could find to help herself stand up. When I got back from the mines and the goulash episode, I had a few weeks' beard-growth and once again Dawn hid under the table and cried her eyes out, she wouldn't come near me until I went and shaved it off. Only then did she recognise me as her dad.

Before we knew it, it was time to organise our possessions – box and crate-up those we were taking back to Blighty, and sell the things we weren't, leaving only what we needed to take with us on the cruise back home. Inside our flat we hung on to Big Bertha until the last possible moment when another family came to carry and shuffle her away to their apartment. I started packing my bits-and-bobs and was looking for the blood-smeared boomerang, could I find it? No! I was gutted. Only when it was too late did I remember what I'd done with it: Dale used to take it to play with his pals and worried he would lose it, one day I hid it under a flagstone outside our block of flats, thinking he wouldn't find it there. I wonder if it was found by somebody else?

The last couple of weeks before sailing were quite stressful what with all the sorting, packing and organising, not to mention the emotional ups and downs of Margaret's farewell work party for herself and Terry. Then there was the last social get-together with Sam and family, and all the visits to and from our friends on camp, and all the farewell gifts we were given. We also had to go visit the Lauro Lines office in Perth to pick-up our tickets and a big wad of documents, and make sure we read and understood them.

And there we were – the final day on camp. Everything packed and sorted, Dale finished at his school, Margaret finished at the hospital, goodbyes said, and lots of promises from friends that they would write (and they did). Only one last thing to do, walk around the camp making one last stop at the office to return three sets of knives, forks and spoons.

Sam, Maureen and their two girls appeared with their ute and car to take us all down to Fremantle. Blimey, that was a sad farewell, everyone, including me and Sam shed a few tears, even Dale gave both girls a hug. It was sad but also a relief to board the *Angelina Lauro,* the ship that would be our home for the next three weeks. We stood on the deck waving to our dear friends below on the quayside. Two horn blasts signalled the start of the voyage, and we continued waving and watching Sam and family shrink into the distance, as we set sail on the Indian Ocean, Blighty bound.

FLOTTA LAURO

LAURO LINES

Head Office:
Via C. Colombo, 45
80133 - Naples

Branch Office:
Piazza Nunziata, 5
16124 - Genova

Copy **E** To Passenger

PASSAGE TICKET

№ 00924

CLASS	Tourist
CABIN	TCP Grade

From FREMANTLE to SOUTHAMPTON

Vessel m/v ANGELINA LAURO Voy. N° 18 Sailing o/a 30th September 196_

Name of passengers	Age	Fares	Sex	Nationality	Amount
JOYCE Mr Barrie Terence	4	1	M	British	$ 383.00
JOYCE Mrs Margaret	4	1	F	"	383.00
JOYCE Mast Dale Gary	9	½	M	"	191.50
JOYCE Miss Joyce Lesley	8th 10th	F	"	38.30	

233

Issued in exchange against the following documents?	Currency collected Dollars	Amount of fares	995.80
	Country where collected Australian	Taxes	5.10
Issued at/on		Total amount paid	$1,000.90

Number	Value
Balance paid	
Address of passenger abroad:	

A G E N T :
FLOTTA LAURO (LAURO LINES)
A/SIA PTY LIMITED

Issued at PERTH on 16/9/6_

Any refunds can only be made in the currency and in the country in which payment was effected

Our precious tickets for our passage back to Britain on the *Angelina Lauro*

The beautiful *Angelina Lauro*

(Image: Copyright SeapixOnline 2023)

CHAPTER 38

The voyage home

When the people on the harbour dock were nothing more than a blur, we went below deck to find our cabin situated on the third lowest of the four decks in the bowels of the huge liner. The cabin itself was very small for a family of four, but somehow felt quite airy and there was even a baby walker ready and waiting for Dawn. Being on the lowest cabin deck we were only one deck away from the powerful engines and the noise of them chugging away filled our cabin. Initially, it was very loud and made sleeping difficult - the noise was almost as bad as the bullfrog's bellows - but day-by-day we got a little more used to it. After one look around the cabin, Dale was away exploring every part of the ship,

"Be careful, son!" I called after him but too late, he was already gone. We later found out that most of the time he was on the top deck, looking out across the ocean.

The *Angelina* was carrying about 800 of us westwards from Australia to various parts of the world. She was a real beaut and effortlessly sailed atop the calm sea. At full capacity she could carry 1230 passengers - about one third of them First Class and two-thirds Tourist Class. I reckon she was about 700 feet long and about 80 feet wide (213 by 24 metres); she accommodated nine decks, including a sports deck with two swimming pools - one for kiddies and a larger one for older kids and adults. Below that deck came the first cabin deck with its own swimming pool, probably that was for First Class only, then below that came the lounge deck with a games room, reading area and a cinema. There was plenty to do on board for adults and children, no excuses to get bored, although I must admit that some of the time, I was.

For the first few days or so the sea was as calm as a millpond, its flat surface broken here and there by dolphins bobbing alongside the ship. The sky was a clear blue and the breeze gentle and cooling. I loved going up onto the upper decks, wandering around and exploring as much as I could and chatting to the other passengers. Thinking back, no wonder Dale was like he was always going off somewhere, he took after his dad! Wherever he went, he was always back in time for the meals, which were provided and included in the fare. The food was pretty good, fresh and varied and we ate with other passengers in the 'Tourist Class' dining room.

PRANZO				DINNER	
		M/n ANGELINA LAURO			
		FLOTTA LAURO			
Zuppe	1 Ristretto caldo in tazza		Soups	1 Hot consommé in cup	
	2 Riso o pastina in brodo			2 Rice or pastina in broth	
	3 Crema di patate Parmentier			3 Potato cream soup Parmentier	
	4 Minestrone alla Toscana			4 Tuscan minestrone	
Piatto di mezzo	5 Pressata di maiale si sott'acceti		Entrée	5 Pressed pork, pickles	
Insalata	6 Mista alla Campagnola		Salad	6 Country salad	
Piatto del giorno	7 Coscie di tacchino alla Cacciatora		Main dish	7 Legs of turkey, Hunter style	
Legumi	8 Macedonia di legumi al burro		Vegetables	8 Mixed vegetables in butter	
		CLASSE TURISTICA			
		TOURIST CLASS			
Tavola Fredda	10 Corned beef Australiano		Cold buffet	10 Australian corned beef	
	11 Insalata di cernia alla maionese			11 Mayonnaise of stone bass	
	12 Carni fredde assortite			12 Assorted cold dish	
	13 Peperoni gialli e rossi			13 Yellow and red peppers	
	14 Olive miste			14 Mixed olives	
Salse	15 Maionese - 16 Menta - 17 Worchester		Sauces	15 Mayonnaise - 16 Mint - 17 Worchester	
Dolce	18 Zuppette Napoletane		Sweet	18 Neapolitan zuppette	
Frutta	19 Mele o Pere		Fruits	19 Apples or Pears	
Bevande	20 Vino - 21 Caffè - 22 Tè - 23 Latte	Giovedì, 16 Ottobre 1969 Thursday, 16th October 1969	Beverages	20 Wine - 21 Coffee - 22 Tea - 23 Milk	

Example of an evening meal ('dinner') menu

One day I was out on one of the upper decks when the *Angelina* sounded three horn blasts at her sister ship – the *Achille Lauro* – sailing in the opposite direction back to Australia; she replied with three blasts. I later read-up about the pair and learnt they'd been bought in the mid-60s by the Italian shipping company, 'Flotta Lauro Line' from the Netherland Line and the Royal Rotterdam Lloyd line when passenger numbers were dropping. They were taken to Italy to be rebuilt and by early 1966 they were ready to sail again. By the time we were aboard the *Angelina* she was only three years out from her rebuild and refit, which explained why everything still looked pretty new and in good condition.

When he wasn't away exploring, Dale got involved in some of the activities put on by the ship's entertainment staff. There was a dedicated play area for the kids with a selection of games available. We had also brought along some books and games to keep Dale occupied in the cabin, thinking that he might get a bit bored, but he seemed happy enough occupying himself and soon made a few pals. Dawn was happy too, chuckling away as she scooted from one end of the cabin to the other, as fast as her little legs would take her in the baby walker.

Every day, Margaret, me and Dawn, we would spend at least an hour on the top deck taking in the fresh sea air and the warmth of the sun. Terry often joined us on the upper decks, her cabin was on the deck above ours and we knocked on her door as we made our way to the top deck. We also regularly visited the noticeboard where it was written how far we had travelled from Fremantle and our next destination and stopping-off point; the first one would be Cape Town, South Africa.

We seemed to be making good progress when suddenly the weather changed, the air on the upper decks became very chilly and the wind was picking up. We felt cold, colder than we had in the last two years and for the first time since we arrived in Australia, I put away my shorts and t-shirt and donned my trousers. The next few days continued the same, which kept us either below decks, confined to the fully enclosed promenade deck, or elsewhere inside rather than outside. Then we noticed we were wobbling and weaving from side-to-side as we made our way through the ship, the lovely calm sea was becoming troubled and quite choppy and then downright rough. At the same time, the sky darkened, bright blue replaced by glowering grey. The rain began to fall. Heavy, heavy rain, followed by thunder and lightning. We had entered a storm.

By the evening of the first day of the storm, Margaret became very sick, she couldn't keep down any food, which prompted me to seek medical help. The ship's staff took me to the doctor who came back to our cabin and diagnosed Margaret to be suffering from seasickness. He gave her some tablets.

An announcement came over the loudspeakers that were dotted around the ship, directing everyone to remain inside their cabins until the storm had passed. But where was Dale? We were worried about him roaming around the ship that was now rolling with the waves, what if he'd gone to the upper decks? I told the crew our son was missing and a couple of them went searching for him, telling me to return to my cabin. Poor Margaret looked pale and green around the gills. Baby Dawn was rolling from one side of the cabin to the other inside the baby walker, chuckling away as her little legs ran as fast as they could to keep up. Margaret tried to swallow the doctor's pills but couldn't get them down and retched them back up again, which made her feel worse. Eventually, she managed to swallow one or two, which gradually began to take effect and made her vomit less, but she hadn't eaten anything for hours and didn't have much left to throw-up anyway.

The crew were gone for about an hour searching for Dale before they returned with him to our cabin. They found him in the dining room, looking through a porthole at the monster waves. What a relief to have him back, I ruffled his hair and told him off at the same time. He said he wasn't scared looking through the portholes on his own. I would have been scared at his age, as I was even then. Being onboard the *Angelina* during that storm was a really bad place to be I was scared for all of us; Margaret was too ill to be scared; Dale seemed to be too far gone into his own dream world to be scared; and Dawn was happy running backwards and forwards with every roll of the cabin. When the crew returned Dale to us, they said that when the sea was calm again, we would be upgraded to a bigger cabin on the next deck up because "it wasn't safe to be down on this level with a baby." Which is funny really because Dawn was oblivious to everything and very happy with the situation.

The storm raged on, and the situation went from scary to terrifying. We were told to secure ourselves to the fixed furniture (e.g. beds, table and cupboard) with anything to hand – belts, pieces of cloth or material, and were even given ropes and straps. The crew checked on everyone hourly or so including through the night. They even brought some food to the cabins, but no-one wanted to eat very much. For 48 long hours we remained confined and bound within our cabins, held hostage by the storm until eventually, the ship's rocking became less violent. We needed to remain secured for a while because an unpredictable swell could easily catch you off-guard and knock you from one end of the cabin to the other. Then the announcement we'd all been waiting for: We had passed through the storm, and soon would be allowed to move about the ship more freely. What a relief that was!

Within twenty-four hours of that announcement the four of us had moved into our new cabin that just happened to be situated next door to Terry's. It was brighter and more airy than our first, and the noise from the engines was less intrusive, although we could still hear them well enough to know they were churning away. The crew continued to bring meals to the cabins because the dining room had been damaged by the storm – it was a good job Dale had been found and brought back to us before that had happened. Margaret was feeling a bit better and was able to eat small snacks again and keep them down. Dale and me, we didn't wander very far because although the storm had passed, there was still torrential rain and we weren't allowed to go out on the upper decks, and besides, it felt better to stay together as a family.

We were settling into our new cabin when suddenly it felt like there was something missing, or that something had changed. Margaret was the first to recognise the missing factor.

"It's the engines, they've stopped!" A second later came an announcement over the tannoy that the engines had been cut due to a broken propeller. We were adrift on the ocean, but only two days away from Cape Town. The crew would work night and day to fix the damage, and help was on its way. This journey was turning into a nightmare experience, but everyone was okay, no-one onboard the ship had been hurt and we were still afloat. Dawn was still chuckling away to herself toddling about in her baby walker, and her baby laughs helped to lighten the mood.

The crew worked like Trojans. They increased the amount of food and drink they brought to the cabins, and when they had time to stop and chat for a minute, they told us that the kitchen had suffered some damage. They also brought cards and games down from the games room to help us pass the time. Margaret was feeling better but still not right and she vowed there and then that she would never venture out on the sea again. Then, just as suddenly as they stopped, the engines started-up again, the familiar and now comforting churning was back with us. Some of the crew had been in the engine room for fifteen hours straight fixing the problem, while others made temporary repairs to the kitchen and dining room. Over the tannoy came another announcement.

"In less than twelve hours we will dock in Cape Town, South Africa." How welcome were those words, to think we would be on dry land again, and for two whole days!

With the *Angelina* safely moored, the passengers were allowed to disembark with the warning to '..stay within the White areas.' What a shock that was - segregation everywhere, even separate benches for white and black people, separate toilets and so on. Terry stayed with us all the time we were on land. At first, we were all a bit nervous and unsure what was what, but we were glad to be on land again, under a lovely blue sky and bright sunshine. It took us a few hours to regain our land legs on our wanderings along the pier and into the city.

We chatted with some of the other passengers heading back to the ship, who told us about a coach trip the following day to Table Mountain. It would also pass the mansion of Christiaan Barnard, the first heart surgeon to carry out a heart transplant from one human to another. After a couple of hours of walking about we returned to the ship and my, what a hive of activity it was. There were cranes and lifts and workmen galore, all beavering away to repair the damage and restore the magnificent liner back to her former glory. It seemed to me that most of the passengers returned to the ship after a few hours, maybe we all felt safer onboard.

For our second day, we went on the coach trip to Table Mountain, and all was going well until we got to the farthest point the coach could reach. The coach pulled into the car park, and the tour guide told us all to go and take a look at the view. Ha! The top of the mountain was shrouded in mist and we couldn't see a thing! On the way back down the mountain, the guide asked the coach driver to pull in to show us many different and interesting places. One of the most impressive was the heart surgeon's home and the grounds the mansion house stood in. One of my strongest memories of that day was of the greenery, the lovely green shrubs and exotic fruit trees. I began to realise it wouldn't be very long before I would see the green, green grass of Yorkshire again!

By the time we got back to the ship, there seemed to be many more people onboard than when we had disembarked that morning. Many new passengers had boarded to sail to the UK. That evening, the crew held a welcome party for the new arrivals and announced we would be setting sail by noon the following day. The engines chugged back into life on schedule. Margaret was feeling a lot better, Dale was back to his wanderings again, and Dawn still chuckled every time she was put in her baby walker. Everything was back to normal.

Bang on schedule we set sail for our next port of call: Tenerife, in the Canary Islands. Before we reached there, came the excitement of crossing the equator. The onboard tradition was to hold a fancy dress party competition for the kids to celebrate the crossing. It was something to do with Neptune, the King of all of the oceans and seas, and when you crossed the equator for the first time it was polite to pay homage to the old duffer, or something like that!

We entered Dale for the competition and although he wasn't happy about it, we thought it would be a good activity to help pass the time. There was a big box full of dressing-up clothes, but Dale didn't like any of them, so Terry and Margaret found a couple of spare white sheets and pinned them together Roman-style to turn him into one of Neptune's helpers. I found a long stick – maybe a broom handle – from somewhere and turned it into a long staff. Hey presto! His costume was complete. Perhaps if he had smiled a bit more and looked like he was enjoying himself, he might have won a prize!

When we had crossed the equator, the *Angelina* was taking us ever northwards. The sun was still shining, and we went outside on the upper decks again. Occasionally, the Atlantic got a bit choppy but nothing like it was during the storm. The dolphins seemed to be enjoying themselves gliding at-pace alongside the liner, and what a beautiful sight they were.

We returned to the dining room for our meals, and since leaving Cape Town a very large South African, black lady wearing very colourful clothes joined us at our table. She had a lovely accent and laughed a lot when we

Not many of the kids look happy taking part in the 'Crossing-the-Equator' competition, including Dale who looks totally fed-up wrapped in a long white sheet!

told her about our adventures. We all became very friendly, and she told us she was on her way back home to London, after paying a long-awaited visit to her parents in Cape Town. My, what a lovely, jolly and interesting person she was. When we told her how we had lived in Australia, she said that no way would that be for her, she was happy in London. She took a real shine to Dawn and loved to hold her hands to help her walk when we left the baby walker in the cabin. Along with Terry, we now had an extended family, and we had a very nice time together for the remainder of the journey home.

Within a week, we were entering the port of Tenerife. We were given a few hours off-ship, which was just long enough for all those passengers leaving the ship to disembark, and for those joining to embark. Our extended family decided to stretch its legs by walking along the harbour, which to me was one of the wonders of the world I had so far seen. There we were, a £10 Pom family and our two friends strolling around the harbour alongside the millionaires and their magnificent yachts. I never thought I would have such an experience!

Later, I learnt that walking along that harbourside, we were only 1900 miles (3060 kilometres) from the port of Southampton, and therefore just over 2200 miles (3540 kilometres) from home. In a few weeks, I would be at work somewhere in Hull while these millionaires would be out on their yachts. At least I wouldn't be under attack from killer spiders, snakes or the burning hot sun, and that would be good enough for me, for now.

Maybe it was the way I felt, or maybe it was real, the closer we got to Old Blighty the happier and brighter the ship's atmosphere became. There seemed to be more singing and dancing in the evenings. Then, before we knew it, the final day of sailing had arrived. The weather was quite pleasant, and the atmosphere onboard charged with excitement. There were a few celebration activities going on, and we all joined in as much as we could for the final few hours of our long voyage. Even Dale had stopped his wanderings and stood with us on the upper deck watching as we sailed by The Needles, the *Angelina* marking this occasion with three blasts from her horn. The three white monster pieces of rock are just off the coast of Land's End and as we passed them all noise onboard the ship stopped; you could have heard a pin drop. The air was full of emotion and tension that was broken when someone shouted.

"Three cheers for Old Blighty!" a call that everyone on the deck replied to.

"Hip hip, hooray! Hip hip hooray! Hip hip hooray!" I have often wondered if that 'someone' calling for cheers was me!

Not long after, we were slowly making our way into the port of Southampton. And that was it – the end of our two-year adventure, which was at times very tough and very worrying but worth it, nonetheless.

We returned to England older, wiser, a bit wealthier and with a new family member.

Thank you, Australia, for giving us the experience of a lifetime!

Epilogue

Within a few hours of docking at Southampton I was driving a hire-car up to Elsie and Bill's house in Hutton Cranswick, Yorkshire. On the approach to Hull, we called at a fish-and-chip shop in Gilberdyke for our tea – our first patties in two years and my, they tasted good!

About two to three weeks later I got a job at Armstrongs in Beverley working at a bench making parts for car jacks. We lodged with Elsie and Bill for about three months until we found a house to buy, and secured a mortgage to top up our substantial deposit from the savings we'd sent back to England.

Dale attended the local village school and complained of the cold, being bored and fed-up because the local kids only ever talked about football, which he wasn't interested in. He was also grumpy because he couldn't go surfing, and once again had to wear his shoes to school! Margaret was busy at home taking care of Dawn.

Shortly after we returned, we got a visit from a government, health department official, 'requesting' Margaret and I take a course of injections for an infection that had broken out onboard the *Angelina*. All of the liner's passengers were tracked down to be given the injections, so whatever they were for, must have been pretty serious. Dale and Dawn didn't need to have the injections and I'm glad they didn't because they were bloody painful, leaving me and Margaret knocked-out and bed-bound for a couple of days.

Then life got onto an even keel, and our Australian adventure faded into the past. We were back into a regular working pattern, buying our own home and looking forward to enjoying its modern features: three bedrooms, an indoor bathroom, front and back gardens too.

Our adventures didn't end when we returned from Australia, there were many more to come but on a smaller scale. Who knows, maybe one day I will get round to writing about them.......